Praise from readers of

Glossary of Terms from
A Course in Miracles

"Words are tools used to convey ideas with which we build concepts. In *A Course in Miracles* familiar words are frequently used with novel meanings developed in the context of the entire work. If you have only one book to support your study of the Course, this is it. Robert is handing us the key to understanding the multitude of concepts developed in the Course. After several years and many false starts of struggling to understand the Course I stumbled onto this work. After a month of 'playing' with this Glossary I felt Robert had 'cracked the code' for me. In my study groups, we still make liberal use of this book. Whether you are new to the Course or involved in advanced study, you will find this book indispensable."
—TIM SCHOENFELDER, M.D.

"I can best describe this book as a brilliant, fresh, and much-needed source for all who have ever used *A Course in Miracles*. Robert is a modern day Teacher of God in the truest sense."
—REV LEE POEPPING, UNITY CHURCH, SANTA CLARITA, CA

"I have found *Glossary of Terms from* A Course in Miracles to be the best single volume to aid in deepening contemplation and understanding of *A Course in Miracles*."
—JONATHAN WILLIAMS, BOULDER, CO

"I want to say how much of a personal and group study Robert Perry's book, *Glossary of Terms from* A Course in Miracles, has been. In my ten years as co-founder of a group in Illinois, we used the glossary for reference by group members, especially as an aid to new members. A particularly nice feature is that of stating the traditional Christian

meaning for a given term, then listing the ACIM meaning of the same term. This is *very* helpful! It is both a compact and a comprehensive aid to Course students, new and experienced."
—BOB RILEY, NEW MEXICO

"I found *Glossary of Terms from* A Course in Miracles very helpful indeed. It has helped me to understand words which may appear easily understood in normal usage but in the Course have a very precise meaning. I would certainly advise anyone studying the Course to have this glossary by their side."
—MATTHEW FORREST

"I am studying alone and have found much of the Text very difficult to understand. Then I found *Glossary of Terms from* A Course in Miracles. What an enormous help it was. To anyone just starting their studies, this glossary is not just useful but essential."
—EWEN CAMERON, SUFFOLK, ENGLAND

"Robert Perry has given us a gift with his glossary. This gem of a Course companion does not get any shelf-time from me. It is always readily available whenever I spend time with the Course. As Robert explains in the introduction, our use of language and the meaning we give to words provide the ego with a comfortable home. The Course, though, uses words we think we understand, and by giving those words different meanings, it transforms our minds. One word at a time, one meaning at a time, our thought system shifts from being ego-centered to miracle-centered. Robert helps to hasten this process and heighten our understanding."
—JAMES ZANT

"We are fascinated with the update to the glossary. As translators, we are in a unique position to see just how closely each word has been studied, explained in each context, and the trickle-down effect it produces in other definitions. A great addition to an already most valuable tool for the serious student, and an eye-opener for newcomers."
—VALERIE MONK AND PATRICIA BESADA, SPANISH TRANSLATORS OF THE GLOSSARY, MILAGROS EN RED

Glossary of Terms from
A Course in Miracles

Glossary of Terms from
A Course in Miracles

Nearly 200 Definitions to Help You Take an
Active Role in Your Study of the Course

Second Edition

Robert Perry

CIRCLE PUBLISHING

Published by Circle Publishing
A division of The Circle of Atonement Teaching and Healing Center
P.O. Box 4238 • West Sedona, AZ 86340
(928) 282-0790 • Fax: (928) 282-0523
E-mail: info@circleofa.org • Website: www.circleofa.org

Cover design by George Foster; www.fostercovers.com
Design and layout by Phillips Associates UK Ltd
Printed in the USA

ISBN 1-886602-26-3

Library of Congress Cataloging-in-Publication Data

Perry, Robert, 1960-
  Glossary of terms from A course in miracles : nearly 200 definitions
to help you take an active role in your study of the course / Robert
Perry.
      p. cm.
  Rev. ed. of: A course glossary.
  Summary: "Clarifies the language of A Course in Miracles, which uses
familiar terms in new ways. Covers all the major, and many minor,
Course terms. In many cases, contrasts the conventional meaning of a term
with the meaning given by the Course"--Provided by publisher.
  Includes bibliographical references.
  ISBN 1-886602-26-3
  1. Course in miracles. 2. Spiritual life--New Age movement.
I. Perry, Robert, 1960- Course glossary. II. Title.
  BP605.C68.P45 2005
  299'.93--dc22
                                    2005011681

Glossary of Terms from A Course in Miracles

These words dispel the night,
And darkness is no more.

Workbook, Lesson 162

Introduction

A Course in Miracles is a modern spiritual path. Designed as an educational program in spiritual development, its aim is to completely reverse the way we perceive the world. As part of this program in changing perception, the Course employs a unique use of language, a use which initially is quite confusing. When the reader first opens the book, he or she notices many terms which are very familiar, yet which do not appear to entirely fit their context; they don't seem to make sense in the way they are used. Since this occurs quite frequently, whole sentences and paragraphs become problematic and confusing.

There is, however, a reason for this confusing habit of the Course. The meaning that we assign to words grows out of the meaning we see in life—in ourselves, in others, in the world. Yet this is the very meaning which the Course wants to transform, the very meaning which clouds our sight and makes us suffer. What the Course does, therefore, is to take the same words we use and fill them with *new* meaning, meaning which expresses the thought system the Course seeks to instill in our minds.

This new meaning will often be a radical transformation of a term's conventional meaning, one that purifies or corrects the ego-based connotations of the old meaning. For instance, the term "Son of God" traditionally implies that only one unique male—Jesus—was God's Son. The Course has transformed this term to one that communicates that everyone—male and female, human and nonhuman—is equally God's beloved extension.

Or the new meaning may be an expansion of the conventional meaning, which makes it a statement about the world as a whole, rather than about just one small part. For example, the word "fantasy" traditionally refers to a specific psychological process in which we entertain imaginary scenarios that we consider more satisfying than reality. The Course broadens the application of this term immeasurably. It claims that this psychological process is responsible for existence as we know it: our thoughts, our behavior, and even the world itself. All of this is our imaginary replacement for true reality.

Or the new meaning may be a deepening of the old, which makes a term into an entire teaching about life, rather than just a pointer to a particular phenomenon. "Anger" normally refers to an isolated phenomenon in our lives, one that under certain conditions is considered to be natural and quite useful. In contrast, the Course views anger as all-pervasive in our lives, as an unjustified, insane emotion that gives rise to our painful condition and that must be relinquished if we are to find peace.

These examples demonstrate that the Course's use of terms is neither careless nor eccentric. The terms and the meanings given them are clearly chosen with extreme care, and great wisdom lies both in the choice of terms and in the new meanings they are filled with. In researching the terms included in this book, I found, without a single exception, that the Course's use of a term was based on a penetrating insight into that word. The Course's author seemed to see before him literally everything about that word, both its essence or root meaning and all the psychological implications of its conventional usage. As a result, the Course will often turn a word's conventional meaning upside down, while at the same time carrying out its root meaning with greater purity and completeness.

Although the author of the Course admits that its terminology is not rigorously consistent on the superficial level, the consistency of *thought* behind a term is truly amazing. As a term is used over hundreds of pages, the various uses provide additional clues into the overall concept behind the term, fitting into it like pieces of a giant jigsaw puzzle. Along the way, the term also interacts with other terms from the Course, playing a supporting role in the overall concepts behind those terms.

The end result is that each term is a study in itself, a teaching in itself. Each term is a miniature container of the Course's entire thought system.

In essence, then, to study the Course, the reader has to learn a new language, and this takes time. Learning this language is quite different from learning a foreign language. For a foreign language uses different words to express the same world of meaning as our language expresses. The Course's language is just the reverse. It uses the *same* words to express a *different* world of meaning. This unique approach to language produces a unique psychological effect. Because the Course's words are familiar, seeing those words on the page triggers their conventional meaning. Yet because these words are also being filled with new meaning, seeing them also triggers the new meaning. Each time a word is used, then, the new and the old meaning arise and meet face-to-face in one's mind. And as they do, the old is slowly shined away by the more compelling and attractive light of the new. Eventually, all the words of the Course *only* trigger—and thus *only* reinforce—the Course's new world of meaning. The end result of this process is that the ego is evicted from one of its primary houses, the house of human language.

This use of language, then, reflects the larger process the Course guides us through, in which our illusions are brought to awareness, where they meet and are replaced by the light of truth; in which we make a shift from the current meaning we see in things to a fundamentally new meaning. If we can replace the egoic meanings contained in our *words*, then we have gone a long way towards replacing the egoic meanings contained in our *minds*. And that is the goal of the Course.

This unique language style not only facilitates the Course's goals, it also reflects the Course's overall philosophy. For this is one of many examples in which the Course operates in the same way it claims the Holy Spirit operates. According to the Course, the Holy Spirit takes forms that we made for ego purposes and assigns to them a new purpose, a new meaning: that of leading us out of the ego. The Course specifically mentions that human language, which was made to disrupt communication, can be reinterpreted by the Holy Spirit to facilitate real communication (T-14.VI.6-7). Presumably, that is precisely what the Course itself has done in its use of terms. And thousands of Course students have experienced the effects of this. They have had their entire outlook on life subtly made over, perhaps without their noticing, by this initially confusing but ultimately transformative use of language. My hope is that this glossary can speed and strengthen this effect in the lives of those students who use it.

About the glossary

I have tried to reflect all of the above in the definitions in this glossary—without going so far as writing a book on each one, which, with many of the terms, would be quite easy to do. Each entry is thus somewhere in between a brief definition of the term and a short essay on the concept. As such, the entries are subjective. They represent my current understandings, understandings which I myself frequently modify. With many of the terms in this book I have gone through several changes of understanding over the years.

For me it is a given that no glossary will ever capture all the fullness and nuance of meaning contained in the Course's terms. Yet still I hope that this one will prove to be a helpful source of understanding, reflection, study, and discussion for students who seek a more complete grasp of *A Course in Miracles*. My hope is that many of the definitions express more clearly what Course students already understand. And so far as I know, many of the definitions are new. Some disagree with understandings which have become accepted wisdom among Course students, yet which, in my mind, do not hold up when researched in the Course.

The following information will help the reader in making use of the entries (not all of the entries contain all of these elements):

Root meaning

In some of the entries the first definition is labeled "root meaning." This represents an underlying or core meaning that both the conventional meaning and the ACIM meaning have in common.

Conventional or Christian meaning

After the term is listed in bold (and after perhaps a root meaning), some entries will first give a *conventional* meaning or *Christian* meaning, before giving an *ACIM* meaning. This is the meaning that in my opinion the Course's use of the term is implicitly playing off of or responding to. This conventional (or Christian) definition does not attempt to capture the entire meaning, but emphasizes the meaning that seems to relate most directly to the Course's, usually by way of contrast. This part will sometimes include comments about the Course's perspective on that conventional meaning.

Boldface words

Words in boldface type refer to other entries in the glossary. They mean "see this word elsewhere in the glossary." In any given entry I have not bolded all of the words that are defined elsewhere in the glossary, only those which pertain more or less directly to the term under discussion.

References

For study purposes, I have tried to include some of the more important Course references to a given term. This, however, is not a main focus of this glossary and so is not done with any kind of completeness. When the reference is in parentheses, this means the reference pertains to the sentence in which the parentheses occur, rather than to the whole entry. When the reference is not in parentheses and comes at the end of an entry, it pertains to the entry as a whole.

All references are given for the Second Edition of the Course and are listed according to the numbering in the Course, rather than according to page numbers. Each reference begins with a letter, which denotes the particular volume of the Course or one of the Course's supplements (T=Text, W=Workbook for Students, M=Manual for Teachers, C=Clarification of Terms, P=*Psychotherapy* supplement, S=*Song of Prayer* supplement). After this letter comes a series of numbers, which differ from volume to volume:

> T-chapter.section.paragraph:sentence
> W-part(I or II).lesson.paragraph:sentence
> M or C-section.paragraph:sentence
> P-chapter.section.paragraph:sentence
> S-chapter.section.paragraph:sentence

Note: In Part II of the Workbook, a "lesson" number from 1 to 14 refers to one of the "What Is" sections, which come at ten-lesson intervals.

Suggestions for using the glossary

Individuals

Apart from the usual uses of such a glossary I have a few suggestions. One will have more appreciation for a term if one not only reads the definition, but also reads the references given, as well as looks up the definitions for the bolded words. One can also make the terms more practical and relevant by asking oneself how a certain situation in one's life would look if one really believed the concept behind a particular term. For instance, you might consider how a difficult interaction you had today would look if you really believed what the Course says about the term "freedom."

Study groups

In addition to individual use of the glossary, I think that study groups might benefit from going over a term, or cluster of terms, a week. As mentioned above, this would be enriched by looking up the references, reading the bolded definitions, and discussing application to one's life.

Studying the Course's use of language is like diving into an ocean. The thumbnail sketches provided in this glossary can barely begin to hint at the depth and breadth of that ocean. I look forward to the day when in-depth studies can be done of all the Course's major terms, along with many of its minor ones (which must number in the hundreds), and even its repeating images and phrases. For now, though, I hope this modest glossary will contribute both clarity and depth to your study of the Course, and will give you a sense of the mastery of this unique tool of spiritual awakening.

Glossary of Terms from
A Course in Miracles

accepting the Atonement for oneself

Accepting the healing of your own thinking, accepting **right-mindedness** into your mind (even if only briefly), which leads directly and automatically to extending **healing** to others. *Accepting* healing is the precondition for *extending* healing, for you must *have* before you can *give*. This acceptance is the sole responsibility of the **miracle worker**, because once Atonement is allowed into your mind, it will automatically extend through you and give **miracles** to others (unless you block it). Thus, rather than implying that others are of no concern to you, this idea tells you *how* you can be truly helpful to them. You can accept Atonement by changing your perception of self *or* others, as well as by joining with your **holy relationship** partner (*see* T-22.VI.4:4-5:3). *See* T-2.V.5:1, M-7.3:2-6.

adjustment

We spend a lifetime adjusting to the **world** and its demands, slowly crafting and fine-tuning an image of ourselves that fits the world and how it sees us, so that we don't stand out (*see* **self-concept**). The world holds a picture of us in which our job is to meet its demands and accept its judgments of us. Adjusting to this picture seems required, simply because the world is bigger than us. We don't realize that our **ego** made the world, and specifically designed it to hold this picture of us, so that we would feel forced to adopt the picture as our own. Instead, we must refuse to adjust to what the world tells us we are. In other words, the last thing we want to be is "well adjusted." Rather than adjusting to the world, we must merely look on **reality** directly, to which we have no need to adjust. For the purpose of any adjustment is to bring two things into alignment that do not fit, and we and reality are inherently a perfect fit. *See* T-20.III.

altar

Conventional: A raised structure on which are performed acts of worship or sacrifice towards a deity.

ACIM: An inner altar, not an outer altar. The place in your mind that contains what you are devoted to, worship, consider sacred. "These altars are not things; they are devotions" (T-5.II.8:7). You have placed the ego's idols upon your inner altar and worshipped them, yet it is God Who really belongs on your altar and Who really is there. Sometimes spoken of as a single altar that is (only apparently) defiled; sometimes spoken of as two altars, one to the ego and one to God. *See* T-5.II.8:5-9, T-11.VI.5:1-2.

angels

Helping spirits from God whose job is to protect our minds from the ego and light our way home. They are often shown attending, protecting, and nurturing the birth of the Christ in us. The helping function of angels is very similar to that of the Holy Spirit, implying that perhaps angels are simply extensions or aspects of the Holy Spirit. *See* W-pI.183.2:2.

anger

The emotion which stems from condemnation, from the **judgment** that someone is not fulfilling the function you allotted her and is attacking you, from the perception that she has sinned and should feel guilty. Anger is expressed as **attack** and results in **guilt** and finally **fear** of punishment. This fear of outer attack seems to justify further anger (*see* W-pI.153.2:1-2), and the cycle starts over. Anger results in guilt and fear because it comes from your unconscious **attraction to guilt** and fear. Behind mild annoyance, anger over specific situations, and anger over certain attributes in particular people lies intense, total, and nonspecific fury (*see* W-pI.21.2-5). "Anger is never justified" (T-30.VI.1:1; *see* M-17.8:6). Even the destruction of the body does not justify anger, for the body is not real. Jesus taught this in the **crucifixion** (*see* T-6.I.4). Anger obliterates your helpfulness, obscures the peace of

God, and is a sure sign that your thinking is guided by the ego. The major lesson of the teacher of God is to learn how to respond without anger to his pupil's egoic thoughts (*see* M-17.4). *See* **attack thoughts**. *See* T-15.VII.10:3, T-30.VI.1:1, W-pI.192.9:4-5.

appearances

The outward or visible form of things. We all know that appearances *can* be deceiving, but the Course teaches that appearances are *inherently* deceiving; they are never true (though some are more reflective of truth—for instance, the physical healing that comes from the miracle). Appearances are forms in constant change, while the **truth** is formless and beyond all change. Our task is to see past appearances to the truth beyond. Every appearance, no matter how seemingly traumatic, can be overlooked. If we look past them, we call forth the **miracle**, which can heal all diseased appearances, no matter how extreme they appear. However, if we think that certain appearances can give us something (which is another way in which they deceive, for they promise what they cannot deliver), then we will believe they are real and cannot be overlooked, and this will limit the power of the miracle to heal them. *See* T-30.IV.5-6, T-30.VIII.1-3.

Atonement

Root meaning: To reconcile or set at one (it thus refers to the *recovering* of at-one-ment, not the *state* of at-one-ment). Specifically, the reconciliation of God and His children, which is achieved by the wiping away of what caused the rift: the children's **sins**.

Conventional: The sins are wiped away by payment for them; in Christianity, by Jesus paying for them on the cross.

ACIM: The sins are wiped away by the realization that they were not real in the first place, and hence that the rift with God never happened. Therefore, Atonement in the Course is said to undo *errors* (rather than sins), correct *perception* (rather than the corruption of one's soul), and *cancel out* past errors (rather than pay for them). "Atonement…enables you to realize that your errors never really occurred" (T-2.I.4:4). Put simply, it wipes away what stands between us and God with the knowledge that *nothing* stands between us and God. Jesus made this principle accessible to us through his **resurrection**, not his **crucifixion** (indeed, the resurrection is sometimes called the Atonement—*see*

T-3.I.7:8—in contrast to Christianity calling the crucifixion the Atonement). This placed him in charge of the Atonement. Atonement is one of the major terms in the Course and has many aspects:

1. It is a *principle*: that the separation (or fall) never really occurred (*see* T-6.II.10:7). In this sense, it is the final lesson.

2. It is a *power* which, when we accept it, comes into our minds and heals our thinking (*see* T-1.I.37, T-14.IX.3:2). The **miracle** is thus the expression of the Atonement.

3. It is a *plan* for the return of all God's sons (*see* **plan for salvation**), a plan based on the Atonement principle.

4. It is a *process*, in which the Sonship progressively approaches the final reunion with God (*see* T-1.III.1:1).

5. And it is a *purpose*—the goal to which the plan and process aspire (*see* T-2.II.6:9).

See **salvation**. *See* **accepting the Atonement for oneself**.

attack

The expression of **anger**, in the attempt to punish others for their sins and defend oneself from their attack. Its true result is **guilt** and **fear** of retaliation. It is the fundamental expression of the ego. It blots out the awareness of Heaven and is the cause of all of our experience of *being* attacked. Exists first on the thought level (*see* **attack thoughts**), from which it may also be expressed physically. Attack is one of the primary purposes the ego sees in the body (since only bodies can actually attack), a purpose which is the source of physical **sickness**. Attack, however, is not real. **Minds cannot attack** each other, for they are joined. And minds cannot be attacked, for they cannot be truly injured. Thus, since it is unreal, attack is never a **sin**. It is merely a **call for love**.

attack thoughts

Thoughts of **anger**. The source of our entire perception of the world. We entertain attack thoughts, then project them onto the world (*see* **projection**), and then interpret the world as wanting to take vengeance on us for our attack on it. A term found only in the Workbook. *See* W-pI.22.1.

attraction of guilt

The ego's desire for **guilt**, which is the unconscious motivation behind all the ego does, including all its uses of the body. Guilt is the ego's only need (*see* T-15.VII.10:4). It finds guilt attractive because guilt preserves it, *confirming* its foundation of sin and *producing* its essence of fear. The attraction of guilt makes God and love seem repulsive. Because *we* find guilt intolerable, the ego promises to relieve guilt, but does so in ways that actually maintain and increase it (*see* T-15.VII.4:1). For instance, the ego urges us to relieve our guilt by attacking others, projecting guilt onto others, and looking for sin in others. If we simply realized that these things only *increase* guilt, we would let them go. This is why we must look at our unconscious attraction to guilt (*see* T-15.VII.3). The solution to the attraction of guilt is the **holy instant**.

authority problem

Conventional: Our problem with other people wielding authority over us, stemming from our desire for self-determination.

ACIM: Our problem with the fact that God is our Author, and our attempt to author ourselves, to usurp God's power, throne, place, or function. This attempt, which we believed seriously attacked or killed God, is the hidden source of all **guilt**. In the separation, we rejected His role as Creator and tried to be creator in His stead. We tried to create our own self and even to create God (*see* T-21.II.10:4). However, we only succeeded in making a self-*image*, the **ego**. Now we believe we can change ourselves (a form of creating ourselves) by modifying our image. A conventional authority problem results from projecting this belief (in self-creation) onto another person, which leads us to fear that he or she can take our function of self-creation away from us and can exercise creative power over us, can modify us against our will. All of this, though, is illusion. Since we did not author ourselves we have no power over what we are, nor do others. We have not usurped God's power and have no cause for guilt (*see* "**I am as God created me**"). *See* T-3.VI.7-8, T-11.In.2.

7

being

That which exists, the "substance" or is-ness of which something is made, the real essence of something. All being is in God, Who created us by sharing His Being with us. Our being is therefore pure **spirit**, without form or limit. Being is absolutely changeless and certain, calm and unshakable. At the same time, however, being is inherently relational. By nature, it must give or extend outward. It gives all of itself away all the time, thereby increasing its fullness. Being therefore is both static (changeless) and dynamic (extending and increasing). You could say it is *statically dynamic*. This is one example of the collapse of conventional dichotomies that occurs in the state of being. Another example is that, in this state, having and being are not different; what we *have* is what we *are* (*see* **having/being**).

body

The dream symbol of the **ego**; a physical wall around the mind that reflects the ego's mental wall; an illusory prison that seems to keep the mind separate from all else.

1. The ego made the body as proof that we really are separate, and that our separateness is outside our power of choice, being enforced by an objective wall of flesh. As a result, deep down we hate the body, blaming it for all the pain that separation brings. We also hate it because we think it is not good enough to be our house.

2. The ego uses the body as a device to reinforce itself. It does so by using it to **attack** others and to seek physical pleasure. It adorns the body to make itself feel special (*see* **specialness**) and to attract special love partners (*see* **special relationship**). It uses the body's **sickness**, aging, and **death** to "prove" to us that we are frail and guilty and that God is dead.

3. The Holy Spirit sees the body as neutral, as having no power over the mind. He sees it as a means not an end, a "means of communication" (five references; *see* T-8.VII.Heading, 2:1, 13:3), an instrument for reaching our brothers with love, forgiveness, and healing. Thus it can be a useful tool here.

4. Yet because it is an illusion, when we awaken in Heaven it will be gone, for there is no form in Heaven.

bridge

A bridge that spans the distance between our awareness and God, between illusions and truth, perception and knowledge. This bridge is variously described as the Holy Spirit, Christ's vision, peace, and forgiveness, among other things. It is described as being built by us, and also built by God. To be literal, it is a transition in our perspective on reality (*see* T-16.VI.7:1). It is described both as the transition to **true perception** and also as the transition to **knowledge**, as the **final step** in which God will bridge the **gap** Himself. *See* T-16.III.8-9, T-16.VI, T-17.II.2, T-28.III.6.

bringing darkness to light, illusions to truth

Bringing our dark, secret, egoic beliefs out of unconsciousness and into full awareness to meet the **light** of the Holy Spirit, of **reason**. There our illusions will be dispelled, for light automatically dispels darkness (*see* T-2.II.1:14). "To bring to" means "to see from the perspective of" or "see in the light of." In other words, that to which a thing is "brought" (truth, light) has authority over the thing which is "brought" (illusions, darkness), authority to define that thing in its image. We have brought **truth** to illusions—seen truth from the perspective of illusions (*see* W-pI.107:5:3-4). Now we must reverse that. Our job is not to bring the light, which would imply that we are separate from the light and it is up to us to make or earn it. Our job is simply to bring our darkness to the **Holy Spirit**, and it is He Who brings the light. We have hidden the ego's darkness behind walls of **denial**, which the Course describes metaphorically as dark doors in our minds, guarded by sentinels of darkness (*see* T-14.VI.2:5, 8:4). Since darkness vanishes automatically in light, it is not our darkness that keeps us from God, but the act of hiding it behind the dark doors. Once we have brought it to light we can fulfill our **function** of bringing light to the darkness of the world, just as the Holy Spirit does (*see* T-18.III.7:1-3). *See* T-14.VII.6, T-14.IX.1-2, T-14.VI.4.

brother

One who is like you and shares the same Father. All members of the Sonship, which includes all living things, are brothers. Sometimes refers specifically to our holy relationship partner, especially in Chapters 17-22 in the Text. By calling us all "brothers," the Course is filling a traditional word that refers only to male siblings with a profound and nontraditional content that embraces all reality (*see* **he, him**). The term "brother" in the Course implies that underneath our apparent differences of gender, culture, age, status, and even species, we are all absolutely the same. It also implies that underneath our worldly relationships as parents, children, enemies, and strangers, we are really only brothers to each other—equal offspring of the same Father. "You have come with but one purpose; that you learn you love your brother with a brother's love. And as a brother, must his Father be the same as yours, as he is like yourself in truth" (T-31.II.10:5-6).

call for love/help

The real nature of **attack**. Attack seems to be a **sin** but is really a call for love or help. When someone attacks us, the attack seems to deprive us. Therefore, we seem to be the one who is in need, and we seem to be justified in attacking to take back the dignity our attacker stole from us. The truth, however, is the reverse. The one in need is the *attacker*, for his attack pushes away from him the very love that, deep down, is his heart's desire. His attack, then, leaves him feeling deprived and in pain. This pain is a call for the love his attack has pushed away, a call for help out of the hole he has dug for himself, a call for correction of his error, and a call for the healing of the sickness his attack represents. We answer this call by giving him love, for that is what he is really asking for. This overall concept takes many forms:

1. Attack is a call for love (*see* T-14.X.7:1-2).

2. Attack is a call for help or correction or healing (*see* T-12.I).

3. What we call sin is merely a mistake or an error (*see* T-19.II-III), a failure to understand (*see* W-pII.359.1:2-3), a lapse into insanity (*see* W-pII.FL.In.5:4-7).

4. Early in the Text, sin is spoken of as a lack of love as opposed to a positive act of evil or assault (*see* T-1.IV.3:1-3, T-5.V.4:10).

See **"mind cannot attack."**

cause and effect

The basic law of mind, the law of **extension**, in which a cause extends itself outward in the form of effects that are in its likeness. By causing effects the cause is proven real and is expanded. Change can only be introduced at the level of cause, not effect. Effects *cannot* turn around and create their cause, as the ego maintains.

1. God is the Cause and His Son is His Effect (*see* T-2.VII.3:11).

2. The ego, however, has tried to reverse effect and Cause, claiming that you, the effect, are your own cause, and that God is actually your effect (*see* **authority problem**).

3. The outer **world** is merely an effect of your mind. The only meaningful healing, then, is to heal the cause, to change your mind.

4. The ego again tries to reverse effect and cause, telling you that the world and the body are your cause and you are their effect (*see* **projection**). It thus counsels you to solve your problems by changing outer situations, circumstances, and other people (*see* **magic**).

5. Because the ego has had no real effect, it cannot be a cause. This is why the ego has no real "dynamics"—it is not dynamic, causative (*see* T-11.V.3).

6. You prove your brother's ego is not real when you show it has had no effect on you (*see* **invulnerability**).

7. When a miracle is caused through you, healing another, this effect becomes a **witness** to the fact that the Cause of healing lies within you.

See "**ideas leave not their source.**"

charity

Root meaning: Generous, liberal giving; giving others more than their seeming due.

Conventional: Generous physical giving or service.

ACIM: Generous perception. Perceiving others in a far more positive light than seems to be their due. Seeing the perfection in others. Charitable or right-minded perception is the source of **miracles**, but does not pertain to knowledge. *See* T-2.V.9-10.

choice

The mind's ability to decide between different alternatives. Choice is truly free. It is caused in each moment purely by the mind itself rather than by the past or anything external. Not even the Holy Spirit knows what we will choose from moment to moment, and He cannot override our choices. Choice is meaningless in Heaven, where only **will** exists; "the concept of choice...is not of God" (T-10.V.14:2). It only makes sense within the **split mind**, which has invented an alternative to oneness and so must now choose between its two allegiances. Real choice is not between outer alternatives (e.g., what to eat, what to wear, whom to marry, etc.), as the ego maintains. Such "choices" are merely smoke screens for the only meaningful choice: the choice of whether to think with the ego or the Holy Spirit. And even this choice is an illusion, for only one alternative is real. Yet by using the illusion of choice to choose only **truth** we eventually remember that only truth is true and thus that no choice exists. *See* T-6.V(C).4:8-10, T-24.VI.7:1-2.

Christ

Christian: Jesus, who is the Christ, the Son of God. *ACIM*: God's extension, His one Son and one creation. Our true Identity; the single Self that is shared by all the members or parts of the **Sonship** (*see* T-15.V.10:10). The second Member of the Trinity; the Holy Spirit abides within Christ as Christ abides within **God** (*see* W-pII.6.3:1). Does not refer to Jesus, who is simply one of these members who has remembered our shared Identity. Christ is fully at one with God, indistinguishable from God, and eternally awake in God. He cannot sleep (*see* T-12.VI.5:4). *See* **Son of God**. *See* T-11.IV.7.

Christ's vision

See **true perception**.

clouds

A metaphor for the dense, chaotic mass of insane thoughts, largely unconscious, which block our awareness from the light of our true nature, yet which have no real substance. These are often spoken of as "dark clouds" or "the clouds of guilt," for they are made of **guilt**. Also refers to the objects and events of this world, which are literally nothing more than this same mass of thoughts in our minds. *See* T-18.IX.6-8, W-pI.41.5, W-pI.69.4-8.

communication

Conventional: The exchange of information between minds through a system of outer symbols such as words.

ACIM: The direct joining of minds, through the extension of one mind to another. "Communication ends separation" (T-8.VII.4:1). Conventional communication is actually pseudo-communication designed to *disrupt* communication.

1. In Heaven, communication is the direct, unmediated, and nonspecific sharing of **knowledge** between all minds. It is also the means by which **creation** occurs (*see* **extension**).

2. The **separation** was a disruption (or failure) in communication. This is the ego's sole purpose for all that it does. The ego invented bodies and human language in order to *not* communicate while *appearing* to communicate.

3. The **Holy Spirit** is "the remaining Communication Link between God and His separated Sons" (C-6.3:1). There is no communication at all between the ego and the Holy Spirit.

4. The Holy Spirit guides us to re-establish communication with our brothers through letting go the blocks to joining (*see* **forgiveness**) and so experiencing our oneness.

5. The Holy Spirit sees the **body** solely as a means of communication. It is a *temporary* communication device, needed because our vision is still dim (*see* M-12.3:3-8). It becomes unnecessary when our minds learn that they can communicate directly without it (*see* T-15.IX.7:2).

6. The **holy instant** is a time in which we give and receive communication.

7. Revelation is direct communication from God, which we at times experience in this world. *See* **communion**.

See T-4.VII.3-4, T-15.IV.8, T-15.XI.7, T-18.VI.8:3-8.

communion

Christian: A sacrament in which bread and wine are partaken as symbols of Jesus' body and blood, in commemoration of Jesus dying for our sins on the cross.

ACIM: **Communication**, the joining or sharing of minds. Jesus states that he would not share his body with us because it was meaningless, and that his death was not a payment for sin (*see* **crucifixion** and **Atonement**). He says, however, that he will share his mind with us, in the holy instant and in the holy relationship. *See* T-7.V.10:7-12, T-19.IV(A).16-17.

consciousness

The conscious part of the mind (conscious-ness), which perceives, experiences, chooses (thus, in the Course, this term does not denote a general principle or substance that pervades all levels of mind). "Consciousness is...the domain of the ego" (T-3.IV.2:2). Consciousness can receive messages from the ego, which is buried in the unconscious, or from the Holy Spirit, Who is also outside the conscious mind. It must choose between these two voices. It can be trained to experience miracles and see the real world. But it is inherently perceptual (subject-object oriented) and cannot reach knowledge. *See* C-1.7.

content

See **form/content**.

course, the

A three-volume book which constitutes a spiritual path. Its title, *A Course in Miracles,* could be rephrased as: an educational program in awakening to God through accepting and extending the healing of perception (*see* **miracles**). The Course's many references to itself contain the following main themes:

1. The purpose of the Course is to teach us to remember who we are, to escape fear and attain complete peace of mind, to bring us to the state of perfect healing immediately preceding the reawakening to knowledge and Heaven (*see* **final step**). It does this not by changing our outer lives or by indulging us in the play of ideas and philosophical speculation, but by training our minds, by leading us to the complete reversal of our thinking (*see* M-24.4:1).

2. The Course is workable and effective. It is simple, direct, perfectly clear, easy, and consistent (*see* T-20.VII.1:3). It asks almost nothing and offers everything. It can be learned, can be learned immediately, and cannot fail.

3. We think it does not work, is not specific enough (*see* T-11.VIII.5:1-4), asks the sacrifice of all we hold dear, and is too difficult to learn. This appears to be true only because our egos are fighting the Course, interpreting against it, trying to discredit it, not doing what it says. We are afraid of the Course *because* it will work, because it offers happiness, guiltlessness, love, God. These things are our deepest fears, yet they are also our deepest desires. If we will just do what the Course says, we will see that it works and become motivated to follow it all the way.

See **curriculum,** **"God's Son is guiltless," thought system.** *See* T-In, C-In.

creation

Root meaning: The act of bringing something real into being. That which is thus brought into being.

Conventional: The act of making or inventing new things in this world: forms, systems, ideas, or works of art. God's creation of the world. The world that He created.

ACIM: The act of bringing into being "new" parts or aspects of transcendental reality. God's creation of **reality**, of the **Kingdom**. The sum total of all that God created. Produces only the eternal (*see* T-8.VI.3:3). Occurs only in **Heaven** (T-17.IV.2:1); in this world we can only engage in **making**. In creation, a Member of the Trinity uses its will to extend its being, its love, "outward" to produce "new" parts of Heaven. These new parts are pure spirit: formless, timeless, perfect, infinite, and whole. They are also completely united with and the same as their creator. Through this process the creator extends itself, increasing in fullness and completion.

1. God created His Son, the Christ, thus extending and increasing Himself. The Son, then, is creation—the sum total of what God created.

2. God gave us the function of creating, and so we extend His creation outward by creating in His Name (we do this in unison with our brothers). This is our true function, to which forgiveness returns us.

3. The Holy Spirit also creates (*see* C-6.1:2).

See **extension, function,** and **creations.**

creations

1. God's creations, which are completely nonphysical. The **Sonship,** which is one, but is composed of an infinite number of parts or Sons (*see* W-pII.11.1:1).

2. Our own creations in Heaven, which we create in unison with God and all our brothers, and which complete us and establish our own fatherhood. Creating them is how we increase the Kingdom and give thanks to God for our own creation. In fact, our song of love to God is simultaneously our song of creating in His Name. These creations, in turn, pour out their eternal gratitude to us for giving them the gift of life. They call to us from Heaven to return to them. They, like everything in

Heaven, are pure spirit, formless, timeless, and perfect (for the one direct description of what our creations are, *see* T-24.VII.7:1-3). Note: They are *not* our extensions or thoughts of love *in this world* (*see* T-17.IV.2:1).

See **creation**. *See* T-8.VI.5.

crucifixion

The symbol of the **ego** (T-13.II.6:1). What the ego does to every Son of God who believes in it.

1. The ego devises a **world** which constantly crucifies us in little ways and finally kills us (*see* T-13.In.2-4). We assume God is using the world to crucify us for our sins. Yet *we* dream the world in order to crucify *ourselves* for our sins.

2. The real crucifixion is inner, not outer (T-13.III.6:4-6). It is the condition of anguish which results from our guilt, and from the ego trying to crucify our true Self, the Son of God within us.

3. We try to crucify others, yet this is precisely what leads to #1 and #2 above.

4. The crucifixion of Jesus.

Christian: A ritualistic transaction with God in which Jesus made himself the sacrifice for our sins and thus paid the debt of our sins.

ACIM: An extreme teaching example of true forgiveness, in which Jesus underwent an intensified version of the crucifixion we all experience, yet did not perceive it as real. The events of the crucifixion themselves had no redemptive value (*see* T-3.I.1:2, T-14.V.10:1); it was how he perceived and responded to them that led to the **resurrection**. His response demonstrated that no attack—no matter how extreme (*see* **no order of difficulty in miracles**)—can truly hurt or kill us, the Son of God. He demonstrated that instead of responding with anger and retaliation we should teach only love (*see* T-6.I).

See **Atonement**.

curriculum

A series of lessons planned to help you achieve a **learning** goal. The ego has a curriculum and so does the Holy Spirit. For both curricula the learning goal is to teach you who you are. Yet they are complete opposites, based on opposing notions of who you are. Following the ego's conflicting, impossible curriculum has made you such a depressed, handicapped learner that you need a special curriculum with a special Teacher (the Holy Spirit). The learning goal of His curriculum is **forgiveness**. This will lead to the **final step** which is beyond the scope of the curriculum. He will gear the curriculum to your very individual needs. Yet it is not up to you to establish the curriculum nor even your particular form of it (your particular spiritual path). *A Course in Miracles* portrays itself as one form of the Holy Spirit's universal curriculum. *See* **course, the**. *See* T-8.I.5-6, T-12.V.5-9.

death

The central illusion, the idea that eternal **life** can be lessened, compromised, can lose vitality and be extinguished. The single idea behind all forms of pain, lack, or limitation. The most stark example of this idea is death of the **body**. Death seems to be the final power in this world, for it overpowers all things in the end (*see* W-pI.163.2).

1. The ego tells us that if death is god in this world, then death must issue from God. It must be His punishment for our **sins**. Therefore, says the ego, we should fear Him.

2. Yet physical death is our punishment of ourselves. We made it ourselves (T-1.I.24:1) and are attracted to it.

3. We made it to give ourselves justification for the **fear of God**. For the ego wants us to fear Him and stay away from Him, since *it* fears disappearing in God's unlimited Life.

4. This fear of God's Life makes the ego want to conquer His threat. It does this by apparently killing His Son, which "proves" that it has defeated, even killed, the God of Life (*see* W-pI.163.5, 7).

5. Death, however, is a complete illusion, for life, spirit, cannot be lessened, killed, or changed in any way. Bodies do cease to function, but do not die since they were not alive in the first place.

6. Since death is not real, physical death does not accomplish anything. It is not a way to escape the pain of life nor a way to get to Heaven (*see* T-6.V(A).1).

7. When we realize that death does not exist, we will be able to lay our bodies down voluntarily when our job here is done (*see* W-pII.294.1:5-10). Or, as with Jesus, our bodies will simply vanish.

See T-19.IV(C), M-27.

defense

1. Our physical defense against outer attacks. This backfires, for it affirms that the attacks are real and that we can be injured (*see* W-pI.153.1-5). Further, the idea of self-defense is simply an excuse to attack and so leads to guilt (*see* **attack**).

2. Closely related to this outer defense is the ego's system of psychological defense (the primary one being **projection**), which also backfires, for it too affirms that what it defends against—internal guilt—is real. **3.** The ego's true purpose behind these defenses is to do precisely what they do: reinforce the reality of outer attack and inner guilt. Reinforcing our fear and guilt is how the ego defends its "reality" and so defends itself against God.

4. Yet to keep our allegiance—to defend itself from being relinquished—it must also offer us "gifts." Its chief defense in this sense (its most boasted gift) is the **special relationship** (*see* T-17.IV.5).

5. The **Atonement** is a defense, which does not attack and does not make real what it defends against (*see* T-2.II.4). For it protects us from illusions by showing us their *unreality*.

See **denial**.

defenselessness

Conventional: Being without a means of protecting yourself from attack, and so being completely vulnerable to harm.

ACIM: The attitude and response that stems from realizing that you cannot be attacked or harmed, that you are invulnerable. It thus comes from strength and leads to safety. Ironically, defensiveness is what lays you open to attack by affirming that attack is real and you are vulnerable. *See* **defense** and **invulnerability**. *See* W-pI.153, M-4.VI.

delusional system

Conventional: A psychological term for a system of exceedingly faulty beliefs about reality that persists despite obvious and overwhelming proof to the contrary.

ACIM: The ego's **thought system**, which is fixed, tightly organized, and apparently stable, yet which is inherently vulnerable because it flies in the face of reality and would fall apart under real scrutiny. The delusions in this system include the idea that we can actually attack God and tear away part of Him (T-5.V.3:9-10) and that we made our own father (T-11.In.2:4).

denial

A refusal to admit the truth of something. The psychological **defense** of putting something unwanted out of one's mind. The "decision not to know" (T-14.I.2:2).

1. The ego's thought system is a denial of **reality**, a refusal to admit the **truth**. This submerges our awareness of reality deep in the unconscious mind (*see* T-11.I.8:1-4).

2. We then deny the raw hatred, guilt, and fear we feel inside (which comes from our denial of truth). This very concealment affirms that we still believe in these emotions. This more common use of the word is found only rarely in the Course.

3. The proper use of denial is not to conceal illusions, but to calmly refuse to admit that they are true, to correct our belief in their reality (*see* T-2.II.1:11-2:6).

4. And since illusions are denials of truth, "The task of the **miracle worker** thus becomes *to deny the denial of truth*" (T-12.II.1:5).

See **dissociation**. *See* T-7.VII.1.

devil

Conventional: A supernatural being who opposes God and is the cause of all that is wrong in the world.

ACIM: The **ego**, the self we made (and think we have become), which opposes God and is the sole cause of all suffering and "evil." *See* T-3.VII.2:4-8, 5:1-4.

dissociation

To separate something from awareness as a mechanism of ego defense. A "decision to forget" (T-10.II.1:2).

1. The mechanism by which the **separation** occurred (*see* T-6.II.1:4-5). The separation was not a physical parting, but a mental decision to forget.

2. The ego then dissociated from God's Answer: the Holy Spirit and His thought system (*see* T-14.VII.4). "Dissociation is a distorted process of thinking whereby two systems of belief [the ego's and the Holy

Spirit's] which cannot coexist are both maintained" (T-14.VII.4:3). They are maintained by keeping them in different compartments of the mind. When they are brought together, one must dispel the other (*see* **bringing darkness to light**).

3. The ego even uses dissociation to keep contradictory goals in its own thought system from coming into contact with each other (*see* T-15.I.4:12).

See **denial**. *See* T-10.II.1.

dream

Conventional: An imaginary experience the mind has when it loses consciousness of "reality" (as in sleep), or when it hopes for something better than "reality" (as in "hopes and dreams").

ACIM: All experiences the mind has within the **world** of time and space, including the world itself, which are simply imaginary experiences your mind has while asleep (*see* **sleep**) in Heaven and unaware of true **reality**. Just like nighttime dreams, this world seems to be reality, seems to exist outside your mind and independent of it, seems filled with things and people that are not part of you, and seems to cause you to feel things. Yet, also like dreams, it is an escape from reality, a **fantasy**, which exists within your mind and was caused by you. Just as nighttime dreams (especially wish-fulfillment dreams) are your protest against the insults of daytime "reality" (*see* T-18.II), so daytime dreaming is your protest against true reality.

1. Conventional experience and states of mind in this world are described as nightmares. These are painful because you seem to be attacked from outside and because you do bad things that seem to warrant punishment. Release comes from realizing that they are only dreams, that you are the dreamer who made them up.

2. You can choose that your nightmares be changed into **happy dreams**, forgiving dreams. From these you can awaken to reality. *See* T-27.VII-VIII.

dream figures

The figures we see in the world. This refers primarily to human bodies, but more generally to all the forms we see. These figures seem to be real and independent of our minds. Believing they are real, we assign them roles or functions, things they are supposed to do to save or protect us. However, they are simply figures in our **dream**. As such, dynamics within our minds are controlling them. They act out thoughts of ours which frighten us and which we refuse to admit are inside us, yet which we still want to hang onto. So these thoughts seem to live outside of us, animating the dream figures. These are often thoughts of self-attack, which is why the dream figures so frequently attack us. *See* T-18.II.5:3-6.

ego

Root meaning: The individual self, as distinct from other selves or the world. *Ego* is Latin for "I," and when you say "I" you are referring to a self distinct from others.

ACIM: The entire self you think you are, the "I" you think you are. This self is false, was made by you, and is actually only a *belief*: The belief that you are a separate entity—a separate mind living within a separate body—that you have your own personal history and future, your own will and private thoughts, that you create yourself and sustain yourself. This is not who you are (*see* **Christ** and **Son of God**) and so the ego is a contradiction, an insane belief (*see* **insanity**), a mistaken identity. The ego is in direct, fundamental, and total opposition to God (*see* **devil**). Its basic mood is **fear of God**, fear that it will disappear into His Love and Oneness. Its single motivation is to protect its "existence" from the "threat" of God and make itself a permanent, eternal reality. Its goal is to conquer and kill God and replace Him on His throne (*see* **authority problem**). To do this it must keep your eternal allegiance (as its maker) while at the same time trying to kill you, since you are God's Son. It hopes to attain this paradoxical goal through persuading you to constantly **attack**. By promising you that attack will bring you pleasure and safety, it keeps your allegiance. Yet it knows that attack will really bring death, since attack makes you think you deserve to die for your sins. The ego, however, is merely an idea, and thus has had no effect on who you really are. It has no power over you and can be relinquished whenever you choose, at which time it will simply disappear, be reinterpreted. *See* **separation**. *See* T-4.II, W-pII.12, C-2.

error

Wrong thinking; a mistake. The original error was the **separation**. All errors are merely splinters or subdivisions of this (*see* T-18.I.4:3). Errors are not real and call only for correction (*see* **call for love/help**). By making them real (*see* **making error real**), they appear to be **sins** that are beyond correction and call for punishment. The ego's plan of forgiveness is to make error real—focus on it, interpret it, evaluate its degree—and then try to forgive it (*see* T-9.IV.4). True **forgiveness** simply looks past error in the first place, responding to all errors in the same way and dispelling all with equal ease (*see* **no order of difficulty in miracles**).

eternity

Conventional: An endless stretch of time.

ACIM: A state which is completely *outside* of time, which contains no past and no future, no beginning or end, only "always"—the single instant of the limitless present, without direction or change. Because there is no change, no disturbance, eternity is perfect **peace**. *See* **Heaven**, **reality**, and **Kingdom of God**. *See* T-9.VI.7:1-3.

extension

The basic law and natural dynamic of the mind whereby **ideas** in the mind are expressed outward (though without leaving the mind), thus causing effects after their nature and likeness. The mind then looks upon and experiences these effects. Through this process of causing effects, the mind's original ideas are reinforced, completed, and increased. In short, the mind's thoughts become its *expression* and this expression becomes its *experience*.

1. In Heaven, God extended His Will, His Love, to create His Son, the Christ (*see* **creation**).

2. In Heaven, our **function** is also to extend.

3. On earth, we extend or project our thoughts outward. The result is that what we think becomes what we perceive and what we perceive becomes what we believe (*see* "**projection makes perception**").

4. Our **function** on earth is to extend **love**, forgiveness, and **healing** to others. Merely perceiving others as forgiven is an extension to them, yet we may also use our **body** to actively communicate this forgiveness.

Through healing them, our own healing becomes reinforced (*see* **giving/receiving**, **savior**, and **witness**).

5. Under the ego, extension is distorted and takes the form of **projection**. Because of this distortion, we do not see the connection between the thoughts in our minds and what we see without. Extension is the umbrella for many of the Course's ideas.

See **cause and effect**, **communication**, **creations**, **"ideas leave not their source,"** **laws**, **making**, **miracle**, **sharing**, **special function**, **teaching**, **will**.

eyes of Christ

Spiritual "eyes" in us which see with **true perception**; the "eyes" through which our true Self perceives. The eyes of Christ see a different world than our physical eyes see. They look past bodies and see the light of holiness. They look past sin and see the **face of Christ**. They look past the **world** and see the **real world**. The eyes of Christ are not just receptors, but also givers. They *bless*, and thus deliver miracles to everything they look upon (*see* W-pII.13.3:2). By using them to see an innocent world, we will ultimately see our own innocence. Called "the spiritual eye" in the early dictation of the Course.

face of Christ

What is seen with Christ's vision, with **true perception**. The final perception, in which you "see" the Christ. Since the **Christ** is the true Self in all things, seeing the Christ means seeing Christ in all things. This is an inner experiencing of the innocence and holiness in all things, rather than a seeing of the face of Jesus or any other kind of visual image. Seeing His *face* means that, since you are still in the realm of **perception**, you are still looking upon the Christ in all things slightly from the outside, and thus seeing a facade, a surface, a symbol. However, soon after seeing His face you will transcend all perception and, in direct, unmediated awareness, will again *know* His *being*. *See* **veil**. *See* W-pII.6.4-5, C-3.

faith

Belief and trust in and loyalty to something or someone, regardless of what appearances may say.

1. God, the Holy Spirit, and Jesus all have perfect faith in us.

2. Now we are faithless. This is not a lack of faith but faith in illusions, in nothingness (T-21.III.4).

3. We are asked to withdraw this faith in illusions and give our faith to the **truth**. Truth will call forth this faith in us if we refuse to use our faithlessness.

4. Faith in the Holy Spirit and in Jesus will give us trust in their teaching, their guidance, and their faith in us.

5. In the **holy relationship**, we are asked to have faith that the relationship will reach the goal of perfect holiness, regardless of how impossible this looks (*see* T-17.V.6-7).

6. Above all, we are to have faith in our brother, faith in his innocence, his holiness, and in his eventual salvation, no matter what appearances he presents to us. Through this faith we accept the miracle, which then brings **witnesses** to show us that our faith was justified (*see* W-pII.13.4).

See **charity**.

fantasy

Conventional: The process of manufacturing an imaginary reality inside our minds, in the hopes that it will meet our psychological needs better than reality, which we assume to be unsatisfying. "An attempt to control reality according to false needs" (T-1.VII.3:4).

ACIM: The Course takes this conventional definition and stretches it to cover all that we normally experience, including our mental life, our perception of the world, and our earthly pursuits (in which we use the body to try to act out fantasies and make them "come true"). All these are attempts to find **happiness** through inventing our own reality. In fact, our primary means for seeking happiness in this world, the **special relationship**, is an externalized fantasy process, in which we pursue a fantasy of love, as well as a fantasy of vengeance on past **shadow figures**. Indeed, all fantasies are a seeking of vengeance (*see* T-16.VII.4:2). This vengeance is projected outward and produces our (fantasy-based) perception of a world that wants to take vengeance on us (*see* W-pI.23.3:4). Thus the world's attack on us is simply our own fantasy. We can be free of it simply by valuing **reality** more than fantasy. *See* **dream**. *See* T-9.IV.10-12.

fear

The expectation of being attacked. The single emotion of the **ego**, the emotion of separation. Fear is a recoil into separation, away from a perceived source of danger. In contrast, love extends in order to join with a source of happiness. "Everyone draws nigh unto what he loves, and recoils from what he fears" (T-13.V.5:4). Fear and **love** are thus opposites and are the only two emotions. Fear, however, exists only in relation to love. Fear, in fact, is fear of love, as well as lack of love, denial of love, and a call for love (*see* T-12.I.8-9). Rather than being the initial cause of other emotions, fear is the end result of a chain of emotions and contains implicit within it all the emotions of the chain:

First, we feel **anger**, which is expressed in **attack**. Then we feel **guilt**, for we interpret our attack as a **sin**. Then we fear the punishment and **death** our guilt says we deserve (*see* T-5.V.3:6-11). Out of our fear, we attack in self-defense, and the chain starts over. Fear is the ego's goal and its essence. The ego must cause fear to perpetuate itself, yet it must conceal from us how fearful we are (*see* T-11.V.8-12). For when we truly look at our fear, we will decide that the cost of the ego is too great, and will give it up. *See* **fear of God**.

fear of God

The final obstacle to peace (*see* T-19.IV(D).1-7), the **veil** across the **face of Christ**, the only thing that keeps us from God. Our fear of God exists on two distinct levels.

1. The **ego** fears God as He truly is; it fears His Love, Life, joy, and peace. It fears Him because it knows that in His boundless Oneness it would disappear. To keep from disappearing, the ego must give *us* reason to fear Him also.

2. Therefore, the ego persuades us to condemn our brothers, so that we will feel guilty, so that we will punish ourselves with pain, sickness, and **death**. Then, through **projection**, we see God as standing at the head of this system of "**justice**." We think that He is an angry god, Who believes in our guilt and seeks to punish us for our sins, and Who should thus be feared. The fear of God will go as we forgive our brothers, and as we realize that the angry god we envision is our own ego (*see* W-pI.196.8-12), and that the true God is One of Love. *See* **fear**.

See T-29.I.1-3, W-pI.170.9-11.

final (or last) step

Our final awakening to Heaven, in which God Himself will lift us home (sometimes depicted in romantic or parental imagery of God gathering us into His embrace; *see* W-pI.168.3:4, W-pI.317.2:5). What fully restores to us the **memory of God**. Our job, with the Holy Spirit's help, is to attain the state of perfect **right-mindedness** or **true perception** in which we retain not a trace of opposition to (or fear of) the heavenly state. Yet even then there will be a **gap** between our perception and **knowledge**, which we cannot bridge. It is God Who bridges this gap, reaching down to lift us into Heaven. He will do this the instant we have no resistance to Heaven—we do not have to wait on

Him or on our brothers. We play no part in this step, because we did not put ourselves in Heaven in the first place. And lifting us back into Heaven is somehow the same act as bringing us into Heaven in the beginning. Thus, the last step was paradoxically accomplished in the first step—our creation by God (*see* T-13.VIII.3). *See* T-7.I.6-7, T-18.IX.10.

forgiveness

Conventional: Giving up your resentment towards another and your right to punish him, even though you keep the perception that he sinned against you and that you are justified in resenting and punishing him. According to the Course, this forgiveness cannot forgive, for it affirms that the other sinned and thus is worthy of condemnation (yours and his own). It also affirms that you are holier than he, because he sinned and you forgave (*see* T-27.II.2:8).

ACIM: Giving up your false perception that another sinned against you and that you are justified in resenting and punishing him. Releasing this perception automatically releases your resentment and desire to punish. Releasing another not from what he did, but from "what he did not do" (T-17.III.1:5), from your misinterpretation of what he did. This can forgive, for it frees your mind of resentment and releases the other from the accusation of sin and guilt. The rationale behind forgiveness is that **sin** is not real. It is a wrong perception of **attack**. Attack has no power to do real harm (*see* "**mind cannot attack**"), because what is real (in you and in your "attacker") cannot be harmed or changed in any way. The ultimate rationale for forgiveness is that "the separation never occurred" (T-6.II.10:7, *see* **Atonement**), that "**I am as God created me**," that "**God's Son is guiltless**." Attack, then, has no effects. It is a harmless mistake, a **call for love**. Thus, what caused you to feel hurt was not the other's attack, but your own misperception of his attack. Forgiveness lets this misperception go. As a result, it heals the other person of guilt, and can even heal his body. It also heals *your* mind of guilt and fear, for these came from your anger and resentment. It also heals you of your sense of separateness, for it takes away the perception of sinfulness that made you recoil from your brother. Forgiveness is the source of **extension** and the way to joining. Forgiveness is **salvation**. It is the central theme of the Course, and (according to the Course) of the Holy Spirit's entire **plan for salvation**. *See* W-pII.1.

form/content

Two aspects possessed by things in this world; the shape (form) something takes—the words, images, or behavior it is clothed in—and the essential meaning (content) which that form is meant to communicate.

1. The ego disregards content, believing that the form *is* the content, the form *is* the meaning. It puts on impressive and complex displays of form, in the attempt to hide its own meaningless, incoherent content (*see* T-14.X.7-9). It thinks that problems are matters of form and that the solution lies in changing the form.

2. The Holy Spirit sees the form as neutral, as inherently meaningless and content-free. Because His only concern is the content, He will adapt the form to suit the need. He communicates the same content through all paths (M-1.3), all teachers (*see* T-14.V), and all lessons (*see* W-pI.193), regardless of differences in form.

3. Our only concern should also be the content. We must realize that what will save us is not a change of form but a change in content, a change in the meaning we see in things. We must see the same content in all choices, events, and situations.

freedom

Root meaning: The ability to express your **will** without any impediment or obstacle; "to do your will" (T-30.II.2:1).

Conventional: The ability of your body to say and do whatever you want without impediment or obstacle (*see* T-22.VI.1-2).

ACIM: The ability of the *mind* to express its will to love and join, without the obstruction of the ego (which is an alien will).

1. True freedom is our natural state in Heaven, where our will to love extends infinitely outward without any hindrance whatsoever (*see* **creation** and **extension**).

2. We are not free to change this native state, only to deny it.

3. This world is a state of imprisonment, in which we seem to be imprisoned by the **body** (*see* W-pI.199.1) and by external circumstances.

4. Yet the real imprisonment here is being a slave, a hostage, to the ego; obeying its alien will. Bondage to the ego results in **guilt**, which is imprisoning, for guilt says we *deserve* imprisonment.

5. In this world our only remaining freedom is the freedom of **choice**

(*see* T-12.VII.9:1, C-1.7:1), the choice between the ego and the Holy Spirit.

6. We find our freedom through freeing our brothers from guilt. Conversely, finding our own freedom enables us to free the world.

function

Our function is **extension**. All guilt and sadness come from not fulfilling this function.

1. In Heaven, our function is **creation**, in which we extend God's function of creation (*see* T-9.III.8:1-5).

2. On earth, our function is **healing** (*see* T-12.VII.4:6-9), which comes from extending forgiveness to others. This is how we reach **happiness**. The Holy Spirit gives us a special form of this extension, which is called our **special function**.

3. The Holy Spirit's Own function is to heal us, to lead us back to God, to return us to eternity.

See **teaching**. *See* T-13.IV.1.

gap, little gap

The space between reality and your dreams, which God will **bridge** in the final step. The space between your mind and your brother's, which is a mental space—"a wish to keep apart and not to join" (T-28.III.4:3)—but is symbolized by separate bodies and the physical space between them. In this imagined gap arises the entire world, which is merely a collection of images projected on the fog that fills the gap. The gap is filled with countless **idols** and is the source of **sickness**. You try to join your brother by having your bodies meet in the gap. Yet real joining comes from acknowledging that the gap is completely empty and is not even there (*see* T-28.VI.5:4). *See* **separation**. *See* T-28.III.3-5, T-28.V.7, T-29.I.

gate of Heaven

An image symbolizing the place of transition from perception to knowledge. We reach the lawns before the gate by reaching the **real world**. Heaven's gate is pictured as always standing open (*see* T-11.IV.6:5-6, W-pII.14.5:5) and as being opened by the key of **forgiveness** (*see* W-pI.193.13:5).

giving/receiving

Conventional: Giving is the opposite of receiving, for what you give you lose (*see* **sacrifice**). Giving, therefore, is usually a subtle way to obligate someone to give you something back, something more valuable than what you gave away (*see* W-pI.105.1-2). The Course calls this "giving to get" (T-4.II.6:5), and says that what is really given in this case is guilt.

ACIM: "Giving and receiving are the same" (this line occurs six times in the Course; *see* T-25.IX.10:6). The real gift is not the physical thing, which you do lose, but the idea of love behind it. And when you give an **idea**, you do not lose it (*see* T-5.I.1-2). Rather, it increases as it is shared with others. Moreover, you will not recognize what you have received until you give it, for giving is the proof of having. Your gift proves that you have an idea and that you deserve to receive it. According to the Course, this is one of its most important and most radical concepts (*see* W-pI.105.3:10, W-pI.126.1, M-4.VII.1:6-8). *See* **extension**, **function**, **healing**, **law of love**, **teaching**, **witnesses**.

glory

Conventional: Exalted praise, honor, beauty. Also, a halo of light surrounding a divine person (such as Christ or God) or surrounding the sun.

ACIM: Exalted praise, honor, beauty. Also, a shining radiance that emanates from **holiness**. Glory is of God, but the Course does not focus on acknowledging it in God. Rather, we need to see the glory that God gave our brother. This will reveal the glory that He gave to us, and allow our glory to shine upon the world, shining away the world's illusions and illumining the minds of others.

God

Root meaning: The supreme Being, the Creator, the Father and the Mother, the Source of all that exists and the Goal of all desire.

Christian: The Creator of this world, Who loves His children yet Whose justice demands that He punish them for the sin of turning away from Him, and Who sent his Son to die for their sins.

ACIM: The infinite, eternal Mind or Spirit, Who creates only nonmaterial spirit, like Himself and one with Him, and Who is only pure Love, without any anger or attack (*see* T-29.I.1:5). God has no gender (*see* **he, him**), no personality, no form (*see* T-18.VIII.1:7), and no boundary. But in some sense He is a Person, for He has Thoughts, Will, and awareness, and feels Love, peace, and joy. However, unlike human faculties and emotions, these are infinite, formless realities that never fluctuate (*see* **Thoughts of God**). God only gives and holds nothing back. His children are His joy and He wills only their **happiness**. To everyone He gives the same gift: all of His Love, all of Himself. This is how He creates, by giving Himself (*see* **creation**). His creations receive all their life, their sustenance, and their joy from Him. The **Will of God** is too powerful to have any opposite or obstacle. Thus, His **laws** cannot be broken. When His children seemed to attack Him and descend into sin and evil (*see* **separation**), He did not reciprocate. He knew they merely fell asleep inside His Mind, though He did not know nor understand what they were dreaming nor who they dreamt they were. Instead of retaliating, He simply gave them His Answer, the **Holy Spirit**, to guide them home. In the meantime, He waits for them with open Arms, yearning for their return. He does not hide Himself, but is totally accessible. He can be known in the direct experience called **revelation**. And when His children have healed their minds and lost all fear of Him He will reach down and lift them home Himself (*see* **final step**).

"God's Son is guiltless"

The Course's own summary of its message, a phrase it calls the central theme of the universal course (M-1.3:5), the one message given to all teachers of God (T-14.V.2:1), and the Holy Spirit's only judgment (M-10.2:9). It means that **forgiveness** is always unconditionally deserved. Even though it seems that everyone is guilty of leaving God and attacking his brothers, no sin occurred and so no **guilt** is justified. Thus, every person is still part of God's one Son, at one with God and with each other, within the safety of His transcendental Kingdom. *See* **Son of God**. *See* T-31.I.7-8.

grace

Root meaning: A pure blessing or a state of pure blessing, given by God, which makes no demand on the receiver, which the receiver must do nothing to contribute to or earn.

Christian: An undeserved gift from God that saves or sanctifies us.

ACIM:

1. The heavenly state in which everything is freely given us and there are no difficulties, struggles, guilts, or burdens (*see* T-7.XI.1-2).

2. The salvation that we receive in the **holy instant** (*see* T-19.I.13).

3. The act of God reaching down and giving us the **revelation** of His Presence, either a) in the form of a temporary experience of divine union (*see* W-pI.169.12:2-3), or b) in the form of the **final step**, in which He permanently awakens us to Heaven. *See* W-pI.168-169.

gratitude

Appreciation for blessings received. The appropriate response to reality and its gifts. An essential aspect of love, which brings joy to those who give it as well as those who receive it.

1. The state of Heaven, the **song of Heaven**, which we sing to God in gratitude for our creation and which He sings to us, in gratitude for completing Him.

2. Here on earth, the appropriate response to God, the Holy Spirit, and Jesus, which they do not need, but which we do.

3. Our proper response to our brothers for what they are, regardless of their behavior (*see* T-12.I.6:2).

4. The response to us of those we heal, by which our healing returns to us (*see* **witness**).

5. The response of God, the Holy Spirit, and Jesus to us for allowing our minds to be saved and for helping Them save the world.

6. Under the ego, we are grateful when others sacrifice to us and when we are better off than others. And we demand gratitude from others lest we withdraw the gifts we gave.

See W-pI.195, W-pI.197.

Great Rays

The Rays of light and holiness that shine out from the Christ within each person. These are lit by a **spark** that God placed in each individual at creation. We begin the journey by seeing our brothers as bodies. Then we at some point begin to see the little spark in them. Then we will see the Great Rays shining out from that spark. We "see the Great Rays shining from them [our brothers], so unlimited that they [the Rays] reach to God" (T-15.IX.1:1). The body will then fade from our sight and we will give up special relationships for relationships without limit. The body will then disappear and we will again know the light of the Rays in direct **knowledge**. Note: The Rays are revealed through **vision**; they are not composed of visible light nor seen through the body's eyes. *See* T-10.IV.8, T-16.VI.4, 6.

guilt

Conventional: The state or status of someone who has broken the legal code, the ethical code, or the law of God (we will call this the state of guilt). An inner experience of the state of guilt, a feeling which says you are bad because you sinned (the feeling of guilt).

ACIM: The emotional experience of the belief that a) because you committed a **sin**, b) you have made yourself into a bad person and c) deserve punishment and **death**. Guilt's ultimate basis is the belief that a) we attacked and separated from God (*see* **separation**), and thus b) murdered our divine innocence and turned ourselves into egos, who now c) deserve death and **hell**. This belief is utterly false, for a) we are incapable of sinning or separating, b) cannot remake ourselves, and c) cannot die. Hence, there is no such thing as the *state* of guilt. There is only the unfounded *feeling* of guilt. Guilt is at the core of our experience here. It maintains linear time, for it rests on *past* mistakes and demands *future* punishment (*see* T-13.I.8-9). It made the physical **world**, which is why the world constantly seems to be punishing us (*see* T-13.In.2-4). It is the essence of our perception of the world. It is the sole cause of all pain. We think that feeling guilt is honest humility which motivates us to obey God's laws. Yet guilt is purely an ego device for arrogantly demonstrating that we are separate from God and should fear Him. Guilt maintains the ego's existence. For this reason, the ego is *attracted* to guilt (*see* **attraction of guilt**). Thus, the ego tells us to "sin" in order to obtain certain pleasures, to attack in order to find safety, and to project guilt onto others in order to rid ourselves of guilt. Yet the real motivation behind all of these, and their real result, is the accumulation of more guilt. Since guilt is the only thing that keeps us from God, the journey home consists entirely of teaching and learning the unreality of guilt through **forgiveness**. *See* T-5.V.

happiness

Conventional: A state of joy, satisfaction, and contentment that is believed to result from possessing or attaining certain outer things or circumstances that one considers desirable.

ACIM: A state of joy, satisfaction, and contentment that results from remembering and extending who we really are.

1. Happiness, being a part of love, is God's Nature and is our natural state.

2. Currently, we have chosen misery instead because we confused misery with happiness. In other words, we do not know our own best interests (*see* W-pI.24).

3. Now we seek outside ourselves for happiness (*see* **idols**) and hold grievances because things do not behave the way we want. This simply yields more misery.

4. To find real happiness, we must realize that we are miserable and that there is no hope of happiness in the ways of the world (*see* T-31.IV).

5. Happiness comes from guiltlessness, which comes from **forgiveness**. It comes not from trying to make things go our way in the world, but from forgiving things for *not* going our way.

6. Happiness comes not from getting, but from giving, from fulfilling our **function** of extending to others (*see* W-pI.66).

7. The function of relationships is "to make happy" (T-17.IV.1:3). The **holy relationship** is one in which the purpose of making miserable has been replaced with the purpose of making happy (*see* T-17.IV.2).

8. God's Will for us is perfect happiness (*see* W-pI.101). Thus we need not pay for it, but merely accept it. Once accepted it is by nature constant, unless we reject it again.

happy dream

A way of experiencing the world that sees the world through the eyes of **happiness**, a state of mind in the world that is totally healed. The concept of the happy dream straddles illusion and reality. Being in this world, it is still a *dream*; yet being *happy*, it is a reflection of **reality**. It is a dream of waking and thus leads to full awakening. The holy relationship, in its mature state, is a happy dream. The happy dream is not a collection of more pleasing external forms. It is a state of mind. Yet this state of mind will often result in healed forms (*see* T-30.VIII.2:5). *See* **dream**, **real world**, **true perception**, **vision**, **right-mindedness**.

having/being

In the world, what you *have* is different from what you *are*. The ego teaches that what you *are* is lacking, empty (*see* **lack**). To be happy, then, you must apparently *have* more. You must acquire things from the outside and make sure you do not give them away. In Heaven, however, having and being are the same. What you have *is* what you are, and what you are is everything. Therefore, you can give all you *have* without losing it because it is not detachable from you, being what you *are*. You remember this state through giving in this world (*see* **giving/receiving**) and through overcoming all doubts about what you are (*see* T-6.V, especially V(B).3, 8, V(C).5-8).

he, him

The Course uses masculine pronouns for all beings: God and His creations (Christ, the Sons of God, and the Holy Spirit). Traditionally, masculine pronouns have been used for both the Trinity (Father, Son, and Holy Spirit—all "He") and the collectivity of humanity (mankind). This has expressed the preeminence of masculinity, the victory of the male in the war of the sexes. The Course, as with so many of its terms, has taken this traditional terminology and filled it with radically new meaning. In the Course, "he" does not refer to the male, nor to specifically male qualities and values. It refers to a spirit that is neither male nor female, neither human, animal, plant, nor mineral, that is beyond all biology and personality and transcends space and time. Thus, rather than favoring one side of the gender gap and affirming the male victory in the war of the sexes, this new meaning does not even acknowledge gender as *real*. For the split between male and female is one of the most fundamental separations, and separation is an illusion. This new meaning further does not regard beings as defined in any way by their bodies, whether those bodies be male, female, human, or nonhuman. Thus, the Course has filled terms which assumed the reality of gender and the preeminence of masculinity with meaning that radically redefines beings as *nonphysical* and *gender-free*. In so doing, the Course marches the new meaning right into the old term, so that the old meaning, with all of its associated scars and aggression, can be brought to light and replaced. *See* **brother**, **God**, **Son of God**.

healing

Root meaning: The restoration of wholeness, the remedy for **sickness**.

Conventional: Sickness and healing are primarily of the body.

ACIM: Sickness and healing are entirely of the mind. The mind's sick thought system is the source of all pain. Healing is thus the replacement of wrong thinking with right thinking; the release from fear and the acceptance of love. The "Holy Spirit is the only Healer" (T-13.VIII.1:2), and the **Atonement** is the principle behind all healing.

1. Healing is not needed in Heaven, where unchangeable wholeness reigns.

2. In this world, the ego tells us that we are beyond the hope of healing (*see* **magic**). This belief, however, is an expression of our underlying *fear* of healing.

3. We ultimately find healing through letting go our perception—of self and others—that we are separate and sinful, which lets us see past sick appearances to the underlying wholeness which has never changed.

4. In this world, healing others is our only **function**, our one true response to all that happens, and our one proper mode of communication. Through **forgiveness** we overlook the sick appearance of others and see their true wholeness.

5. This extension of healing to the minds of others can heal their bodies, yet this is only a shadow or symptom of true healing.

6. Only through allowing healing into our own minds can we extend healing to others (*see* **accepting the Atonement for oneself**).

7. Healing and joining go together. Healing comes from and results in the joining of minds (*see* **holy relationship**).

See **teaching**.

heart

The inmost center of one's mind or oneself. It does not, in the Course's usage, have connotations of feeling as opposed to thinking. In the Course, "heart" and "**mind**" are always paralleled and never contrasted (e.g., "Love cannot be far behind a grateful heart and thankful mind"—M-23.4:6).

1. Most references refer to the innermost center of one's *separated* mind, the place that contains our most central thoughts and feelings. It contains what we *really* think, feel, desire, and value, as opposed to what we like to *believe* or *say* we do; these self-deceptions do not enter into our heart. Thus, the "prayer of the heart" asks for what we really want (even if what we want is things of the world), as opposed to what we *claim* we want. ("What do you ask for in your heart? Forget the words you use"—W-pI.185.8:2-3.) The heart is also where we carry the real experiential effects of believing in the ego. As a result, our heart tends to be tired, heavy, hard, and uncertain. Our heart holds hatred within it, feels terror striking at it, and feels the mark of death upon it. Yet the goal is for it to be transformed. We need to lay different thoughts on our heart, hold different goals to it. We need to become pure in heart, kind in heart. We need to open our heart to God and let Him come rushing in. Then, our heart can be renewed. It can be glad, thankful, at peace. Peace can shine out from it and onto others. It can be stirred, can sing, and be lifted up, and will finally leap into Heaven.

2. Underneath this changeable heart is what you might call our *true* heart, which has never changed since God created us. And so the peace of God still abides in this heart. The **Word of God** is written on this heart. And God Himself dwells within it.

3. Finally, the Heart of God is the inmost center of God. This is what we will enter into and disappear in when we awake. This is where we truly are now. This implies that, rather than being peripheral to God, we are at His very Center, in His very Heart.

Heaven

Conventional: The dwelling place of God, where He lives in perfect and everlasting communion with His children, who enter this state of perfect joy after physical death.

ACIM: The dwelling place that God created for His Son, where They are joined in perfect oneness and eternal peace, where They ceaselessly sing Their song of love to each other (*see* **song of Heaven**). Our home, in which we were created and which we never left. In contrast to conventional images, Heaven is **reality** itself, the *only* reality, and is a realm of pure spirit or mind, without space, form, perception, or change. There are no clouds, thrones, beards, harps, or wings. There are no bodies or passage of time. There is nothing but the pure oneness of Father and Son. "Heaven is not a place nor a condition. It is merely an awareness of perfect oneness" (T-18.VI.1:5-6). *See* **eternity** and **Kingdom of God**. *See* T-13.XI.3,6.

hell

Conventional: The opposite of **Heaven**. An afterlife realm where sinners are eternally punished and forever separated from God.

ACIM:

1. An afterlife realm of eternal punishment which is not real, yet which is the ego's goal for us, and which the ego tells us awaits us after death because of all our sins (*see* T-15.I.3-7). This threat of hell is the unconscious source of all **fear** of the future.

2. This **world**, which, like hell, is a state of separation from God in which we seem to be constantly punished for our sins.

3. What the ego tells us Heaven is, because there we will find God's wrath (or so it says) and there the ego will disappear.

holiness, holy

A quality of divine innocence or purity, untainted by the slightest sin, guilt, or impurity. A quality that comes from God to those things that are like Him. Holiness is the natural condition of God's creations and is shared. It is characterized not by separation from the impure (as in some traditional notions), but by oneness with all things. It can never be tainted or lost, only obscured. Salvation comes through overlooking all unholiness and seeing again the native holiness in others and in oneself (*see* **vision**).

holy encounter

An encounter between two people in which salvation is given and returned and mutually shared. The Course teaches that such encounters are the most powerful catalysts for our awakening, for it is in these that "salvation can be found" (T-13.IV.7:7). It also teaches that the Holy Spirit arranges all human encounters, making sure that each one contains the potential for being a holy encounter (*see* M-3.2). The term itself is seldom used (*see* T-8.III, T-13.IV, P-2.I.4), but the concept occurs throughout the Course (*see* for instance, M-3.2, P-3.III.6, W-pII.315.1, W-pI.95.15, P-2.VII.8).

holy instant

A moment in which we temporarily set aside the past and enter into the present, in which we momentarily transcend identification with illusions and recognize what is real. We enter the holy instant not by making ourselves holy, but by forgetting our normal frame of reference, with its absorption in the past, the future, the body, and our own sinfulness. This allows our minds to be still and shift into another state of mind. There we experience the lifting of the barriers of space and time; unawareness of the body; the sudden feeling of **peace**, joy, and love; recognition of our true **holiness**; and **communion** with all that seemed to lay outside of us—with all our brothers and with God. In this instant we may be bumped ahead years in our spiritual development, because we experience the endpoint of development (*see* T-1.II.6). After this instant we will go forth in time carrying a permanent quiet center of timelessness. Our goal is to eventually make every situation a holy instant so that our lives become a permanent holy instant. At that point we will go beyond time into the endless instant of **eternity** (*see* T-15.IV.6:3). The Course speaks of various kinds, degrees, and functions of the holy instant (which is called an "out-of-pattern time interval" early in the Text; *see* T-1.I.47:2):

1. The holy instant is the birthplace of the **miracle** (*see* T-27.V.3). In it our thoughts are healed and this healing then extends out to the world (*see* T-28.I.11).

2. The holy instant can go beyond the miracle and be a **revelation**, a direct experience of God.

3. We will often bring illusions into the holy instant, making the experience a weakened version of the holy instant (*see* T-16.VII.7).

4. We can experience a kind of quasi-holy instant (which may lead to a true holy instant) through joining with music, a beautiful scene, a memory, or even an abstract idea (*see* T-18.VI.12).

5. The holy instant is the answer to the **special relationship**.

6. Joint holy instants (ones experienced mutually with another person) are the Course's special means of shortening our spiritual journey (*see* T-18.VII.6:3-4). Joint holy instants both initiate the **holy relationship** (*see* T-17.V.1) and are crucial tools in its development (*see* T-18.V.6-7).

See T-15.

holy relationship

A relationship in which **holiness** has entered (also called a "real relationship" in T-13.X and T-17.IV), though this holiness may not yet be fully manifest and the relationship may still be dominated on the surface by patterns of **specialness**. The source of **salvation** (*see* T-20.VIII.6:9), a necessary means to salvation, the Course's special means for saving time (*see* T-18.VII.5-6). The holy relationship is a *process*, a gradual reversal of the **special relationship**. It begins when two or more people truly join in a common goal, at least for an instant (*see* **holy instant**). In this instant, the Holy Spirit enters the relationship and heals it at a deep, unconscious level, changing its goal from sin to holiness. As the two forgive each other, this deep-level healing then slowly works its way to the surface, overturning the remaining ego patterns. As the holy relationship matures, the two will experience an increasing sense of oneness, which will prove to them experientially that they are not separate egos. And they will exercise their joint **special function** of together giving healing to the world. The Course and its supplements mention several forms of holy relationship:

1. The Text (*see* Chapters 17-22) discusses a holy relationship between peers.

2. The Manual discusses a holy relationship between a spiritual teacher and his pupil (*see* M-2.5).

3. The *Psychotherapy* supplement discusses a holy relationship between therapist and patient (*see* P-2.In.4, I.3, II.5-9).

4. The *Song of Prayer* supplement mentions a holy relationship (by concept but not by name) between people who pray together (*see* S-1.IV.1-3).

5. The Text discusses a holy relationship between people who had already had a special relationship (*see* T-17.V.2:2).

6. The Manual mentions that a holy relationship can begin when two individuals first meet (*see* M-3.2:6-8).

Holy Spirit

Christian: The third person of the Trinity, Who is the active Presence of God in human life.

ACIM: The third part of the Holy Trinity (*see* T-5.I.4:1), God's Answer to the separation, the Voice for God, our internal Teacher, the **Communication** Link between God and His separated Sons, the **bridge** between knowledge and perception. God created the Holy Spirit at the **separation** and placed Him inside every sleeping mind as the call to awaken (*see* T-6.V.1:5-2:1). He dwells in our **right mind** and our **Christ** Mind. He has the **special function** of undoing the separation so that God's children can come home. At the heart of everything He does is the fact that He is completely aware of both **reality** *and* **illusions**.

1. This enables Him to translate reality into a form we can understand in the world of illusions. He translates knowledge into true perception, waking into happy dreams, Heaven's laws into laws of mind that operate on earth (*see* **extension** and **laws**).

2. This also enables Him to translate everything we made into a way out of what we made. He translates the world into a teaching device for leading us home, the body into an instrument of communication, memory of the past into memory of the timeless present, our defenses against truth into defenses against illusion, our special relationships into holy relationships, our desire to be special into our special function, human language into a meaningful communication about truth, and so on.

3. He is able to see illusions in **light** of reality, thus seeing their unreality. He sees everything we see, all the pain, guilt, and death, yet realizes that none of it is real. Thus He sees that we are still God's guiltless Son.

4. He can communicate with us who believe in illusions and can thereby lead us to reality. He is our Teacher, Who teaches us **true perception**, guides us into it, and replaces our perception with it when we are willing to let ours go. He judges for us, separating out the true from the false for us. He selects our part in the plan of the Atonement, shows us what it is, guides us in the doing of it, and carries it out through us. When He has led all of God's children home, He will have completed His **special function** and will remain with us in Heaven to keep us from separating again (*see* T-5.I.5:7).

See T-5.I-III, W-pII.7.

humility

Conventional: Seeing ourselves as lowly, sinful, and unworthy (the root of the word is *humus*: earth or dirt). This, says the Course, is false humility or arrogance, for it says that we know who we are better than God does.

ACIM: Realizing that on our own we know nothing, and so instead accepting God's definition of us as His infinitely glorious and holy Son (*see* W-pI.152.9), and accepting His definition of our function as being a savior of the world (*see* W-pI.61.1-3).

"I am as God created me"

The central lesson of the Workbook, repeated in three separate lessons (W-pI.94, 110, 162) and in every lesson of a twenty-lesson review (Review VI). In essence it means that no matter what you think you have done, from the original separation at the dawn of time, through the seeming eons since, and throughout the entirety of this lifetime, you have not changed your original innocence, nor ever can. You still shine with the perfect innocence you had the moment you were born from the Mind of God, for you are still in that moment and always will be. Therefore, nothing is stopping you from going back home. Similar in meaning to "**God's Son is guiltless**," and "the separation never occurred" (T-6.II.10:7).

idea

A representation or formulation produced by the mind. Everything, in the world and Heaven, is an idea. Ideas may be true or false, wrong-minded, right-minded, or one-minded.

1. The ego is composed of mad ideas, false ideas. The ego itself is merely an idea, not a fact (*see* T-4.II.2:6), which is why we can be free of it.

2. All physical forms, including the body, are produced by ideas, being merely the outward reflection of ideas.

3. Unlike physical forms, however, ideas can truly be shared (*see* T-5.I.1-2). Instead of dividing them, sharing ideas reinforces and increases them (*see* **giving/receiving**). The sharing of ideas is how minds can unite.

4. The title phrase of each Workbook lesson is referred to as an idea (as "the idea" or "today's idea" or "the idea for the day").

5. Heaven itself is composed of ideas. The Holy Spirit, eternity, love, joy, and we ourselves are all ideas, and thus can be infinitely shared. Heavenly ideas are far beyond the tiny, changing notions we call ideas. They are not subjective pictures of reality, but are **reality** itself (*see* **Thoughts of God**). Even God is an idea (*see* T-15.VI.4), though He is not an idea conceived by some other mind. The word "concept" in the Course is very similar to the word "idea," though, unlike ideas, concepts stop short of Heaven. For the word "concept" emphasizes *our* making, our *conceiving*. Thus, concepts are generally of the ego, and though they can reflect reality, they must be finally transcended in order to once again know the limitless ideas of Heaven.

See "**ideas leave not their source**."

"ideas leave not their source"

The key concept that thoughts cannot leave the mind that thinks them. This means:

1. As **Thoughts of God**, we cannot leave His Mind, we cannot separate from Him (*see* T-26.VII.13:2).

2. Our own thoughts of separation did not leave our minds and thus had no effect on reality.

3. The world we made has no existence independent of our thoughts and so cannot govern our existence nor cause us to feel pain (*see* W-pI.132.5). To change our experience, then, we must change our thoughts, not the world.

4. The ego says that we can direct **attack** or project guilt outside our minds and escape the attack and guilt ourselves (*see* **projection**). Yet these ideas remain within our mind and are reinforced (*see* T-26.VII.14).

5. When we give an **idea** to others we do not lose it. It stays in our minds and becomes reinforced (*see* **giving/receiving**). Thus, forgiving others makes us feel more forgiven.

See **cause and effect** and **extension**. *See* W-pI.167.3-5.

idols

A false god, which we worship, believing it holds our salvation, but which has no life and therefore no power to answer our prayers or fill our need.

1. The **ego** itself and the **ideas** necessary to its survival—such as sickness (*see* T-10.III.4), weakness (*see* W-pI.92.4:7), cruelty (*see* W-pI.170.6), death (*see* W-pI.163.4), and specialness (T-24.III.2)—which we have placed on our inner altar and worshipped.

2. Any external thing—body, place, substance, possession, situation, achievement, right—that we think will give us salvation by making us special (*see* **specialness**) and by protecting us from danger. We seek these idols to fill our lack and make ourselves complete, and they seem to work for a time. But they always fail and end up being harsh gods that punish and demand but do not give. In seeking them we end up reinforcing our beginning premise: that we are lacking. The reason is that we are unconsciously *seeking* lack, incompletion, and death (the ultimate lack of life). Idols may seem powerful but they are simply toys we made.

See T-29.VII-IX, T-30.III-V.

illusion

Conventional: Something that seems real but is not. A belief about or perception of reality that is false.

ACIM: The Course expands this common definition to include anything outside of Heaven, anything that is imperfect, finite, or painful. This includes any object, situation, or event in the **world** of **time** and space, including time and space themselves. It also includes, and mainly refers to, the majority of our thoughts, beliefs, and perceptions while in this world. These are false perceptions of reality, which we dimly recognize as false, yet which we intensely desire and so try to make true (*see* T-1.IV.2:2, M-8.2:3-4). **Truth** and illusion have nothing in common; we must choose one or the other. The ego tells us that our only choice is between illusions, deciding which ones we like best. Yet the Holy Spirit teaches that all illusions are equally unreal (*see* **no order of difficulty in miracles**) and that all must be brought to truth where they will vanish (*see* **bringing darkness to light**). **Forgiveness** is an illusion, but it is the only illusion that leads to the end of illusions, rather than breeding more. *See* **dream, fantasy**.

impossible situation

The kind of situation into "which the **ego** always leads" (T-9.V.7:1), a situation that is so insane that it cannot work and cannot even *be*.

1. The ego has led us into a situation that is so impossible that it cannot be real. How can we actually split with God (M-13.7:10-13)? How can it be true that "the perfect must now be perfected" (T-6.IV.8:5)? Yet we now believe that these impossible things are possible.

2. The ego always leads us into situations that cannot work. It tells us to forgive others by overlooking the sin we have first made real, an obvious impossibility (*see* T-9.IV.4:1-5). It places us in a situation in which there are so many problems that we can never solve them all (*see* W-pI.79.5:1-3). We need to learn how to get out of this mess, but we are so handicapped that we find it impossible to learn the lessons that will actually get us out (*see* T-12.V.5:1-4). This is why the world is depressing, because the whole *world* is an impossible situation. Yet we can develop our abilities and follow our Guide to the point where we can actually get out.

"I need do nothing"

The principle which states that we do not need to do anything to make ourselves holy, to be worthy of salvation. We need simply let go our active interference and accept the Atonement, and salvation will be given us. Indeed, in the separated state we *can* do nothing (T-8.IV.7:3) and *have* done nothing—that is, have not sinned. To experience the **holy instant**, then, we need not prepare ourselves, for we are worthy *now*. But we do need, for a moment, to *stop* all doing, both physical and mental, and enter a moment of stillness in which past, future, and the body are forgotten. *See* **accepting the Atonement for oneself**. *See* T-18.VII.

insanity

Conventional: A deranged state of mind in which one has lost touch with reality and retreated into a senseless, disordered, private world.

ACIM: The state of everyone in the world who believes in the ego's **thought system**, and has therefore lost touch with true **reality** and retreated into a senseless, private world. In this state you are totally isolated, you think you are someone other than who you are, you fear love and love fear, you hear and speak to **shadow figures** that are not there, you see only the projection of your own split mind wherever you look (*see* T-13.V.6), and you believe your magical wishes have overthrown the Will of God. The ego is based on the insane notions of sin, anger, attack, guilt, defense, sacrifice, punishment, fear, and death (*see* W-pII.12.2). The **world** is a projection of this insanity (*see* T-14.I.2:4-7). From the ego's perspective, God and His Love, peace, and joy are insane. It tries to convince you that He made this insane world and so is Himself insane. Knowing you cannot lead yourself out (for you are insane) God answered the ego's insanity with a sane Answer, the Holy Spirit. The Holy Spirit is the reference point from which you can look back on insanity and see it as insane (*see* T-13.III.6-10). He will give you **reason**, the solution to insanity, which leads the partially sane to complete sanity (*see* T-21.V.8:8).

invulnerability

Our natural condition of being unable to be hurt, injured, or changed in any way, which the **Atonement** restores to us. Vulnerability comes not from being attacked, but from our own **attack thoughts** (*see* W-pI.26.2-4). These assume that we can attack and so can also *be* attacked. These also cause **guilt**, which affirms that we *deserve* to be attacked. Invulnerability, then, comes not from self-**defense**, but from guiltlessness, which comes from being both harmless and helpful. Through **defenselessness**, through teaching our brother we are immune to attack, we prove that our brother is innocent, for his attack did not hurt us. We show him this through our lack of emotional upset (*see* T-14.III.7) and through a healthy body (*see* T-27.II.5:6-9). For upset and sickness are messages we send to our brother which say, "Behold me, brother, at your hand I die" (T-27.I.4:6). *See* **crucifixion**.

Jesus

Christian: The only begotten Son of God who came to earth to die for our sins. We receive salvation through having faith in him and his sacrificial death.

ACIM: One of God's Sons, equal to all the rest, who was the first to perfectly complete his part (his **special function**) in the **plan for salvation**, and so became the leader in that plan and the manifestation of the **Holy Spirit**. Our model for decision, thought, learning, and rebirth. In his life he perfectly demonstrated the way home through true **forgiveness**. In his **crucifixion** he taught that even in the most extreme attacks we cannot be hurt and so can teach only love. In his **resurrection** he set in motion the **Atonement** and brought us all home. Yet we think we are still here, and so he is now a living presence in all minds, who works to bring us to the realization of the homecoming that has already occurred. As part of this function, he has authored *A Course in Miracles* (*see* **course, the**). "This course has come from him" (M-23.7:1). Through its words, he speaks to us, teaches us, and guides us home. He calls us to join with him, but only so that we can receive his love, his faith and trust in us, and his liberating teaching, and so that we can extend his love to the world. *See* T-1.II.3-5, T-31.VIII.7-12, W-pI.rV.In.6-9, M-23, C-5.

judgment

The mental process of trying to decide what things are, which things are desirable and worthy, and which are dangerous and guilty. This results in rewarding and selecting certain things and punishing and rejecting others (*see* T-3.V.7:4-8). On this process rests our perceptions, our emotions, our attitudes, and our behavior.

1. This process does not apply to **reality**, which is all one and is given. Reality can only be accepted and known, not judged.

2. Judgment is the process by which we make and organize our illusory worlds, surrounding ourselves with those illusions which we think will support our egos. We apply this process to people, judging which ones deserve special treatment (*see* **special relationship**) and which ones deserve punishment (*see* T-15.V.7).

3. Judgment is meant to make us safe, but it really brings separateness, guilt, fear, and the impossible burden of trying to play God (*see* M-10.6).

4. Judgment is not our function (*see* T-14.X.5:8-9). It should be given to the Holy Spirit, Who will tell us what things mean and what we should do. He sees only one difference: the difference between reality and illusion (*see* M-8.6). He thus separates all things in the world into those that reflect reality and those that reinforce illusion.

5. The right use of judgment is to judge the ego and decide it is both undesirable and untrue (*see* T-4.IV.8:6-8). *See* **Last Judgment**.

See T-3.VI.

justice

Root meaning: A principle of fairness which says that everyone should receive only what they deserve. This must be assessed based on an impartial account of how well they have conformed to the law.

Conventional: A principle separate from love which punishes sinners for their crimes, taking vengeance on them. A process of deciding who is the guilty one and taking from him to give back to the innocent.

ACIM: A principle which gives **love** and **forgiveness** to everyone with complete impartiality and without limit, which gives no punishment and asks no penalty. This is true fairness because no one has broken God's **laws**. Everyone is still the Son of God, still innocent. Thus, the miracle is *everyone's* just due (*see* **no order of difficulty in miracles**). The world's justice is really *injustice*. It is simply a justification for attack, and all attack is unjust. It also makes us believe that God's Love is separate from His justice, which makes Him seem fearful (*see* **fear of God**). *See* T-25.VIII-IX, M-19.

Kingdom of God

The domain over which God is Father, Creator, and Source; the realm established, maintained, and pervaded by His Will. **Heaven**, **reality**. Not an earthly realm, condition, or stage in history. Rather than within you, God's Kingdom *is* you—you both *have* it and *are* it (*see* **having/being**). It is your right. You are a priceless part of it and cannot be lost to it. It is your Kingdom too, in that you are a creator in it as well.

knowledge

Root meaning: The condition of having certain awareness of what something is.

Conventional: Being aware of or possessing information and concepts.

ACIM: The heavenly condition of knowing **reality** through direct and total union with it, unmediated by physical senses or mental interpretation. Knowledge and **perception** are mutually exclusive, for perception involves a separation between subject and object, knower and known. This makes certainty impossible. Yet knowledge is completely certain and without question. Thus it does not change and hence it is timeless. It is total, having no degrees. In it each part *is* the whole. It is completely nonspecific, abstract. It contains no opposites, no contrast and no comparisons. It cannot be learned, for learning applies only to perception, where information enters from the outside. It can only be remembered. This happens after we reach the state of **true perception**, which contains no opposition to knowledge. The goal of the Course is readiness for knowledge, not knowledge itself (*see* T-18.IX.11). *See* T-3.III-V, T-5.I.6-7, T-6.II.7.

lack

The faulty belief that we are incomplete, inadequate, less than, or empty. We blame our supposed lack on what the world has done to us and try to fill it by gaining the world's **idols** (*see* T-29.VII.4) and its acknowledgement of our **specialness**. Yet lack is caused by our own belief in separation, which causes us to feel lonely and cut off. Lack is solved by realizing that we are not separate and are already complete. *See* **having/being**. *See* T-22.I.1:6.

Last (or Final) Judgment

Christian: A final judgment by God of all souls in which He judges which souls are worthy for Heaven and which get condemned eternally to **hell**.

ACIM: A final healing (rather than a final punishment), in which *we* judge all of our *thoughts*, deciding which are false and which are true, rejecting the false and retaining only the true. This judgment is done through us by God's Voice based on His proclamation that "what is false is false and what is true has never changed" (W-pII.10.1:1) and based on God's Final Judgment that we are still His holy Son, forever sinless, changeless, and pure. The Last Judgment is a collective process (yet individuals can apparently pass through it before the Sonship as a whole enters it; *see* T-2.VIII.2:8), immediately following the **Second Coming** and immediately preceding the end of the world and the **final step**. *See* T-2.VIII, T-26.III.4, W-pII.10, M-15.

last step

See **final step**.

law of love

The law that you can only *have* love by *giving* it. "What I give my brother is my gift to me" (W-pII.344.Heading). "As you bring him back, so will you return" (T-11.IV.3:6). We should live by this law and see ourselves subject only to it, rather than subject to the laws of time (W-pII.277.1:2-6). For the law of love gives to us, while the laws of time take away. Found mainly in Workbook Lessons 344 to 349. Also called the "laws of love" (T-13.VI.12-13) and the "law of God" (T-7.VII.2:5). See **laws**, **giving/receiving**.

laws

Conventional: A rule which governs the way things work. A standard which one must obey or suffer painful consequences.

ACIM:

1. God's laws are the laws of love. They do not demand; they give, guaranteeing **freedom**, happiness, safety. They give everything to everyone. It is not a sin to disobey them; they cannot be disobeyed. The law mentioned most often is the law of **extension**, or **cause and effect**, in which thoughts extend outward, creating after their own nature.

2. This law of creation becomes translated in the dream (by the Holy Spirit) into the basic law of mind or perception: Our thoughts extend outward and determine how we perceive and what we experience (*see* **projection makes perception**).

3. The laws or premises by which ego thinking operates. The ego's laws are laws of sin, which, if obeyed, result in imprisonment, punishment, and death. The ego demands obedience to them, but can only punish those who obey its laws. These are not real laws but laws of chaos (*see* T-23.II), of lawlessness.

4. The laws of this world—physical, social, and religious—are projections of the ego's laws. They are laws that limit, imprison, and kill us. Yet they are fictional (*see* W-pI.76). They only have power over us because of our belief in them.

5. Extending healing to the minds of others is a reflection in this world of God's laws, translated by the Holy Spirit into a form we can understand. These miracles transcend the laws of this world, overturning all the physical laws of space, time, distance, mass, and magnitude (*see* T-12.VII.3:2-3).

6. In the **holy instant**, the ego's laws are suspended and we

experience God's laws of love and freedom.
See **justice**.

learning

Conventional: The acquiring of facts and information. The Course criticizes this definition: "It is hard to teach the mind a thousand alien names, and thousands more. Yet you believe this is what learning means" (W-pI.184.5:2-3).

ACIM: The acquiring of the fundamental **thought systems** that guide our thought, perception, feeling, and behavior. An ability developed by the ego which is used by the Holy Spirit to free us from the ego. Primarily refers to the learning of the Holy Spirit's thought system of miracle-mindedness, which is the learning goal of this course in miracles. Toward this goal the Holy Spirit uses the world, time, the body, the miracle, the holy instant, and the example of Jesus as learning aids or devices. To achieve this learning goal requires the unlearning of everything we now believe. "Properly speaking it is unlearning...that is 'true learning' in the world" (M-4.X.3:7). *See* **curriculum** and **teaching**.

lesson

Either the content of instruction, the vehicle of instruction, or the period of instruction.

1. The **ideas** (content of instruction) the ego tries to teach us, called "dark lessons" (*see* T-14.XI.4-5). The central lesson in these is that God's Son is guilty.

2. The ideas the Holy Spirit tries to teach us as a correction for the ego's lessons. His single lesson—the essence of all His lessons—is forgiveness, or the idea that **God's Son is guiltless**.

3. The situations in our lives (vehicle of instruction), which the Holy Spirit uses to teach us His lesson that nothing outside us can hurt us, disturb our peace, or diminish our love (*see* T-31.VIII.3:1).

4. In the Workbook, the idea for the day is sometimes called the lesson, for it is the *content* we are supposed to learn that day.

5. The whole Workbook lesson is sometimes called the lesson, for it is the *vehicle* for that day's **learning**.

6. A practice period is at times called a lesson, for it is the *period* in which we learn. ("These practice sessions, like our last review, are centered round a central theme with which we start and end each lesson [each practice session]"—W-pI.rVI.In.3:1.)

level confusion

Confusing the three levels of **spirit, mind,** and **body** by thinking that correction applies to a level other than mind. Spirit needs no correction, for it cannot be in error and cannot be tainted by the errors of the mind. The body cannot make errors (since it has no volition of its own) and has no power to hurt the mind or make it happy. The mind is the only level that needs correction—the correction of its faulty thinking. **Magic** represents level confusion and the **miracle** is the means of undoing it (*see* T-2.IV.2). This term only occurs in the first two chapters of the Text. *See* T-2.V.1.

life

Conventional: A principle or force that characterizes a functioning, animated body; biological vitality.

ACIM: A principle or force of spiritual vitality, existence, reality, which is imparted by God, is infinite and eternal, is all one with no separate parts, has no opposite or degrees, and cannot be extinguished or lessened in any way (*see* **death**). "An eternal attribute of everything that the living God created" (T-4.IV.11:7); "the one condition in which all that God created share" (W-pI.167.1:3). Life is of the mind and spirit. It has nothing to do with the body. "There is no life outside of Heaven" (T-23.II.19:1). The body does not live; it has only an illusion of life (*see* T-6.V(A).1:3-4). Life is: "eternal" (T-1.III.2:2), "creation" (T-11.In.1:6), "God" (T-14.IX.4:4), "peace" (T-27.VII.10:5), "thought" (W-pI.rI.54.2:3), "communication with God" (T-14.IV.10:6).

light

1. A spiritual quality of holiness, life, truth, and joy. God created us *in* light and *as* light. Light is thus the substance of our being. The light He placed in us at our creation has seemingly been obscured by the fog of the ego, but it cannot really be obscured. We need to get in touch with this inner light. Once we do, it will radiate out from us and shine away the darkness in other minds, as we see past their bodies to the light in them. Illumining their minds will then make us more aware of the light in us.

2. The light of mental clarity, which makes true **vision** and understanding possible, and automatically dispels the darkness of ego, illusion, ignorance, confusion, sleep, and dreams. Rather than interpreting things in the dim light of our ego, and seeing things in many lights, we need to see everything in the Holy Spirit's light. We need to bring our ego's darkness out of unconsciousness and into His light (*see* **bringing darkness to light, illusions to truth**). And we need to let His light—which is found in us, in our brother's holiness, and in forgiveness—light our way home, so that we do not lose our way in the dark.

See **glory**, **Great Rays**.

lilies

Christian: Symbols of Easter, of Jesus' resurrection.

ACIM: Symbols of forgiveness, for in the Course's teaching, the recognition of innocence is what leads to **resurrection**, and forgiveness is the recognition of innocence. Thus, the Course calls lilies "the white and holy sign the Son of God is innocent" (T-20.I.2:1). When you forgive your brother you are giving him lilies rather than thorns (which symbolize the crucifixion that comes from guilt), placing them on his inner **altar** and thereby placing them on your own as well. *See* T-20.I-II.

little willingness, a

All we need to have in order to receive the miracle and the holy instant from the Holy Spirit. If we give Him a little willingness, as well as recognize our unwillingness, the Holy Spirit will add to our gift His perfect willingness and God will add His unlimited Will. How much is a *little* willingness? A little willingness to receive the holy instant means "recognizing that you want it above all else" (T-18.IV.1:4). A little willingness to have the Holy Spirit remove our wrong thinking means that we want Him to take it *more* than we want to keep it (*see* T-25.VIII.1:6). Thus, having a little willingness seems to mean tipping the scales—wanting what is of God *more* than we want other things. *See* T-16.VI.12, T-18.IV.

living things

Denotes all living things on earth, which seem to be physical or biological entities, but which are really parts of God's one Son and are still as God created them. In other words, their true nature is the same as ours. Despite their physical appearances, they are infinite, eternal spirit, part of God and one with us. They are blessed by our forgiving thoughts and in turn recognize the Christ in us (*see* W-pI.156.4-5). Since the word "living" here does not fundamentally refer to biological life (*see* **life**), "living things" seems to include not only animals and plants but waves, wind (*see* W-pI.156.4), streams (*see* W-pI.109.6-7), and grains of sand (*see* T-28.IV.9).

love

The single emotion of Heaven, which contains within it the emotions of peace and joy. The opposite of **fear** (though in truth love has no opposite). The single dynamic of **Heaven**: "Love is extension" (T-24.I.1:1); "To create is to love" (T-7.I.3:3); "love is sharing" (T-12.VIII.1:5). In love we view something as so attractive, so compatible with us, that we go out to it, give ourselves to it, and join with it (*see* T-18.VI.12:4-5). Primarily refers to Heaven, though occasionally refers to the right-minded state on earth. We can love only like God, for only His Love is real. This means that real love is total, always maximal, without degrees, distinctions, or selectivity (*see* W-pI.127.1). Special love, which is doled out differently to different people at different times, is not love. Love cannot be learned, it need only be welcomed. This is done through **forgiveness**, which is an earthly form of love (*see* W-pI.186.14:2). *See* **creation**, **extension**, **special relationships**, and **meaning of love**.

magic

Conventional: The use of supernatural power to do something that is impossible according to the laws of nature. This something can be either real (as in sorcery) or illusory (as in stage magic). In sorcery, a mere spell, which should be powerless according to natural law, can (supposedly) exercise power over a person. In stage magic, an illusionist can *seem* to cause an impossible effect (e.g., causing someone to disappear), when actually he has produced only an *illusion* of that effect.

ACIM: Any power that purports to produce an effect that is impossible according to the real laws of the universe—God's laws. God's laws cannot be broken, and so this power, like stage magic, can only produce an **illusion** of that effect. More specifically, magic is the power to *save* (or heal) that we ascribe to our own separate self, to certain special people (*see* T-7.V.3-4), or to various external things, such as physical medicine (*see* the list in W-pI.50.1:3). These powers have no real power to save us, for salvation is of the mind and comes from a change of mind. Like the stage magician, all these devices can do is rearrange illusions and thus produce an illusion of salvation. Somewhere inside we know this, and so we only turn to magic when we believe that **healing** is impossible. From the Course's standpoint, a doctor using medicine to cure the body is a magician using magical powers and potions to produce an *illusion* of healing—an illusion because what has been healed (the body) is illusory and what is real (the mind) remains unhealed. However, turning to such magic can sometimes be the best approach due to our high level of fear of true healing (*see* T-2.IV.4, T-2.V.2:5-6). One can divide magic into roughly two kinds

1. Using external agents (such as physical medicine) to rearrange external conditions (such as the condition of the body).

2. Using the mind itself to directly rearrange external conditions, but without a real change in perception.

The Course contrasts magic with the **miracle**. Whereas the miracle is the power of God circumventing the laws of this world, magic is the power of the ego trying—unsuccessfully—to circumvent the laws of God.

magic thoughts

Thoughts which claim that we can be saved by our own separate will, by certain special people, by various external things—by anything other than the **miracle**, the Will of God healing our minds. The **teacher of God** will encounter magic thoughts in his pupils and must learn how to react to them without anger. Found only in Sections 17 and 18 in the Manual. *See* **magic**.

making

The unreal counterpart of creating, the process by which we produce illusions. Whereas *creation* uses an undivided will to produce eternal reality, *making* employs a divided or split mind and produces uncertain, ambivalent illusions. Everything produced outside of Heaven—thoughts, perceptions, forms, and events—is *made*. It is thus unreal and impermanent. The Course occasionally speaks of the Holy Spirit making illusory reflections of reality (*see* T-25.III.4-5). *See* **creation**.

making error real

Believing in the reality of your brother's **errors** or mistakes (in essence, his attacks on you). This makes those mistakes seem like sins. We do this by focusing on, interpreting, analyzing, or resisting them. The ego's plan of **forgiveness** (followed by the **unhealed healer**) is to then try to forgive or dispel these "real" errors, but this is impossible, for reality cannot be dispelled. "To perceive errors in anyone, and to react to them as if they were real, is to make them real to you" (T-9.III.6:7). Does not refer to making the error of the separation real; the phrase "making *the* error real" does not appear in the Course.

meaning

The purpose, significance, or nature of something; how it relates to or affects the larger whole. The real sense or import of a communication. Real meaning is of God and can only be understood in direct knowledge, in Heaven. Our own real meaning is part of God's meaning; we can only know our meaning by knowing God's. We cannot understand real meaning while in this world. Our attempts to interpret meaning will always obscure it. The Holy Spirit, however, can convey to us a reflection of true, heavenly meaning. He can tell us what the people and situations in our lives mean. He communicates meaning in whatever form we can receive. He can be flexible with form because He sees no meaning in it and ultimately disregards it (*see* **form/content**—content being a synonym for meaning). The ego, on the other hand, destroys meaning. It breaks things into separate pieces, substituting chaos and fragmentation for meaning, whereas meaning consists in wholeness, in a unified relationship between parts and the whole.

meaning of love

Although the Course says that the meaning of **love** cannot be learned, only known, it does attempt to teach us a kind of love that reflects love's real meaning. We learn this love in the **holy instant**. Conventional love is characterized by **specialness**; we dole out love selectively to certain special people. We look on someone and decide whether to love that person, in what way, how much, when, and what other feelings to mix in with that love. This is not to know the meaning of love. The meaning of love is that love is one: united within itself and unopposed by a second. In other words, real love loves everyone with the exact same love, and it knows no other feeling, no other response. It loves someone without deciding if he is worthy. It loves him with the same love it gives everyone and everything, without distinguishing him from others. It loves him without limit and without change, with a love that is unaware of any other feeling but love. To love in this way is to know the meaning of love. *See* W-pI.127.1-5.

memory of God

Our remembering of the heavenly state of oneness with God; our awakening to that state. The final encounter with God in which we fully

71

and permanently know Him again, as well as remember our own Identity again (*see* W-pII.304.2:3). Not a memory of past events, but of a present state which is still within us but is denied (*see* T-28.I.4:1-2). This memory can be experienced in holy instants of **revelation** (*see* T-28.I.11:4-12:2), and begins to rise in our minds as we near the end of the journey (*see* T-19.IV(D).1:3-5). But it fully and permanently comes only in the **final step** (*see* W-pI.168.3), after we have looked on the **face of Christ**.

mind

The aspect of the self that includes the faculties of awareness, volition, thought, and emotion. (mind in the Course is not purely intellectual, but includes qualities we would associate with the **heart**). Mind is completely nonphysical; it should not be confused with the physical brain. Mind's true nature is one with **spirit**. Yet, unlike spirit, mind can temporarily fall into error, **sleep**, or illusion (*see* **level confusion**).

1. When capitalized, refers to the Mind of God, of Christ, or of the Holy Spirit.

2. In lowercase, refers to the separated mind, or **split mind**, the mind we currently use. This is the part of our total mind that has fallen asleep and dreams of separate existence. As such, it is in *substance* part of reality, part of God (*see* W-pI.35). It will awaken in God when it is fully healed and continue in creation. Yet its *form*—its appearance of being a separate mind with a separate will, private thoughts, and changing emotions—is the **ego**, an illusion that will disappear when we awaken.

3. In lowercase, occasionally refers to the heavenly mind of a Son of God.

See C-1.

"mind cannot attack"

A basic principle concerning the nature of mind. Minds may seem able to attack each other, yet they cannot. For they are all united, and attack assumes the collision of separate objects. Minds also cannot truly *be* attacked, for this assumes injury, and minds cannot be injured, being changeless. Bodies, however, are both separate and changeable. They *can* attack and be attacked. Identifying with the body, then, makes the mind seem capable of attack. When the mind wants to attack, it directs the body to act out the attack. This produces guilt, which the mind then projects upon the body, blaming the body for its actions. And this causes physical **sickness**. Despite this illusion, mind still cannot attack. This means **attack** is not real, which means **sin** does not exist (*see* T-19.II.1:4-5). *See* T-18.VI.3-6, W-pI.161.6.

miracle

Conventional: A divine healing of the physical world or body, in which the normal earthly laws of sickness and death are momentarily suspended, the Spirit enters, and brings instantaneous healing in ways considered impossible.

ACIM: A divine healing of human *perception*, in which the normal "laws" of egoic thinking (based on guilt, fear, sickness and death) are momentarily suspended. This is carried out by the Holy Spirit, Who shifts our perception from false to true and thereby grants us unconditional, instantaneous, and free deliverance from the imprisoning (yet illusory) problems of this world, regardless of their seeming size or gravity (*see* **no order of difficulty in miracles**). Contrary to our thinking, miracles are truly **natural** (*see* T-1.I.6). They are the opposite of **magic**, where we try to use an unnatural power (something apart from God's Will) to save us by rearranging illusions (rather than awakening the mind to truth). Miracles are the means for achieving the goal of the Course. They bring us to the remembrance of Heaven, where they become functionless.

1. The Holy Spirit will heal our own perception whenever we give Him permission, which we do by suspending our wrong thinking and desiring right thinking (*see* **little willingness, a**).

2. The primary usage is the act of the Holy Spirit extending *through* our mind to heal the mind of *another*. This occurs when we are at least momentarily in a state of **right-mindedness**, when we see a brother free of the past, guiltless (*see* **accepting the Atonement for oneself**). This can result in the healing of his body, and the transcending of all physical laws (*see* T-12.VII.3:3)—though this is a symptom of the miracle, rather than its goal. This will also heal our own mind. Miracles can have unrecognized effects, and in fact affect the entire Sonship. However, we should actively give them only where guided to by the Holy Spirit. Ideally, they should be involuntary—activated through us by the Spirit.

3. A minor usage is God's creation of His Son (*see* T-13.VIII.6:5).

See **extension**, **forgiveness**, **function**, **healing**, and **holy instant**.
See T-1.I.

miracle receiver

Usually called simply "the receiver." One who receives **miracles** from a **miracle worker**. These miracles come from the **right-mindedness** within the worker and are designed to *restore* right-mindedness to the receiver. They also give strength, love, spiritual progress, and conviction to the receiver. To maximize reception, the miracle should be expressed in a form that is most helpful and least fear-producing for the receiver. *See* T-2.V.3:2-3.

miracle worker

One whose function is to allow the Holy Spirit to heal the minds of others through him. One who gives **miracles** to **miracle receivers** (*see* T-2.V.3:2). His task is to deny the denial of truth in the receiver (*see* T-12.II.1:5). To do this, he must first accept the Atonement for himself; he must be in his own right mind, however briefly (*see* **accepting the Atonement for oneself**). He must also ask which miracles he should perform and must trust that once a miracle has been given it has been received, whether it has been consciously accepted or not. He must understand the fear of release (*see* T-2.V.1:1) and cooperate with Jesus (*see* T-2.V(A).17:2).

Name of God

The Course (especially in Lesson 183) asks us to call upon God's Name, but does not tell us what that Name is. The next lesson even says, "God has no name" (W-pI.184.12:1)—apparently meaning that there is no word that is *the* Name of God. Presumably, then, we can use a name of our own choosing. Indeed, Lesson 67 instructs us to choose names for God, asking only that those names are "in accord with God as He defines Himself" (W-pI.67.2:7). The sample names given are "Holiness," "Kindness," "Helpfulness," and "Perfection." Similarly, Lesson 282 says, "Father, Your Name is Love" (W-pII.282.2:1). The most commonly used name for God in the Course is "Father." The Course emphasizes that our true name is God's Name, since we are His Son (*see* W-pI.183.1). The various names we give people imply that each person is separate and unique, whereas, in truth, everyone is part of God and thus has only one Name—His. The Course often speaks of us or the Holy Spirit doing something "in the Name of God," which means to do something on His authority or at His bequest, something that is in line with God's Nature and Will. The Course speaks of us forgiving, being patient with, and giving miracles to our brother in God's Name. And it speaks of the Holy Spirit doing everything that He does in God's Name.

natural

Root meaning: What is in harmony with the nature of a thing or of reality.

Conventional: What we find easy, effortless. What is in accord with the world of (physical) nature.

ACIM: What is of God, since the true nature of everything is God's nature. Heaven, formless abstraction, is our natural state (*see* W-pI.161.2:1). On earth, what is truly natural are **miracles**. The ego, the body, and the "natural" world are extremely unnatural. They are habits we taught ourselves with great difficulty over millions of years. As a result, they now seem natural, while what is truly natural seems alien and difficult. *See* T-16.II.3, W-pI.41.8:1-3.

"no order of difficulty in miracles"

The first principle of **miracles** (T-1.I.1) and of *A Course in Miracles* (*see* T-2.I.5:5), a central part of what miracles mean, "a real foundation stone" of the Course (T-6.V(A).4:5). Though the world is made of problems (sicknesses, pains, fears, etc.) of different shapes and sizes, the miracle can heal all of them with equal ease. This stamps the miracle as being from beyond this world. The Course gives three rationales for why there is no order of difficulty in miracles:

1. The power of God, the power of love, is always maximal (*see* T-14.X.6:12-15).

2. All sons of God are equally worthy of the gift of healing (T-5.VII.2:5).

3. All **illusions** are equally unreal; all are different sizes of zero (*see* M-8.5). The illusion that one problem is harder to heal than others is produced purely by our preference for that problem (*see* T-26.VII.6), our valuing of it (*see* M-8.3:7), which leads us to withhold it from the Holy Spirit's **healing** (*see* T-17.I.3:1). This idea that some illusions are more valuable than others is the basis for the first law of chaos (*see* T-23.II.2).

One-mindedness

The heavenly state of **knowledge**. The word "One" implies that there is no **split mind** and no separation, no distinction between subject and object (*see* **perception**), and no opposite. One-mindedness is reached through right-mindedness, yet is also beyond it. For **right-mindedness** corrects or overlooks **wrong-mindedness**, which never happened. This makes it both inherently dual (not one) and ultimately illusory. *See* C-1.6.

peace

A state of rest, contentment, and fulfillment, characterized by the absence of war, conflict, anxiety, guilt, fear, and want.

1. The state of **eternity** or **knowledge**, the peace of God, in which there is eternal stillness and perfect freedom from danger, war, guilt, or lack. The peace of God rests on the fact that His Will has no opposite. This peace, when first discovered, is entirely unlike all previous experiences.

2. The state just short of Heaven which is the goal of the Course (*see* T-8.I.1:1-3), the precondition for remembering knowledge. Through forgiveness, we relinquish all guilt and attack. This brings about a peace which is not knowledge, but does not attack or obstruct knowledge. It thus allows knowledge to flow into our minds.

3. The ego tries to obstruct peace, for the ego is sustained by attack, by war, and by guilt.

See M-11, M-20.

perception

The process of trying to know an object while separate from it, by interpreting or judging information received by our physical senses. Also, the interpreted images that result from this process. Necessarily involves a separation between subject and object, between us and what we are trying to know. It is thus inherently uncertain (as well as partial and changing) and outside the realm of **knowledge**. It seems that outer things and events themselves produce our perceptions of them, yet our perceptions are actually produced by projecting outward our own belief system, especially our self-concept (*see* **"projection makes** perception"). How we perceive the world determines our experienced condition, and this perception is our **choice**. Healing perception is the goal of the Course.

1. The ego engages in false or upside-down perception. This sees the world of form and time as real, interprets that world as guilty and attacking, and thus justifies emotional responses of fear and anger.

2. The Holy Spirit teaches us **true perception**. This makes way for the final step in which God will lift us from perception to knowledge.

See **judgment**.

plan for salvation, plan of Atonement

God's plan for our awakening, conceived at the moment of the separation and given to the Holy Spirit to carry out. It is guaranteed to work, for it was accomplished the instant it was conceived, even though its accomplishment seems to be in the distant future. Jesus has been placed in charge of this plan, for he was the first to perfectly fulfill his own part.

1. In content, the plan is to forgive, to overlook illusions (*see* W-pI.99.4-6), to let go our belief that others have sinned.

2. In form, this plan is applied to each person very individually, to suit his particular needs.

3. Each person is given a part in this plan (*see* **special function**). His part is essential to the plan (*see* W-pI.100); the whole plan depends on it. His part is to forgive and heal those who are sent to him. The plan thus uses those who are more awake to release those who are more asleep (*see* T-1.III.3:3), and so is called "the plan of the teachers" (M-1.2:10).

4. The plan includes all needed specifics for each individual, specific contacts to be made, specific decisions for each situation. It guarantees that we will be in the right place at the right time (*see* W-pI.42.2). It allows for no accidents.

5. It, in fact, includes a script (written by the Holy Spirit) which covers our entire journey through time and space (*see* W-pI.158.4:2).

6. To receive God's plan, we must let go of our plans. The ego's plan for **happiness** revolves around holding grievances, which are emotional demands that others change so we can be happy (*see* W-pI.71.2-4). This is the opposite of God's plan of forgiveness. Our plans for the future are defenses against the Holy Spirit's plan for us, and block us from finding

our part in His plan.
See **Atonement**, **Will of God**.

practice

Systematic, repeated mental exercise aimed at internalizing the Course's thought system. This practice is primarily taught in the Workbook. Doing this practice entails dwelling on **meaning** and applying that meaning to ourselves and to persons, events, and situations in our lives. This usually involves the slow and focused repeating of words provided by the Course, though some practice involves holding a nonverbal intent aimed at experiencing meaning beyond words.

practice period

The period of time in which we do our **practice**. These periods range from mere seconds to a half an hour or more, depending on the Workbook's instructions for a particular practice period. Also called "exercise period" and "practice session."

prayer

Root meaning: Asking God. Communicating with or communing with God.

Conventional. Asking God to supply us with external things, people, conditions, and events that we think will protect us and satisfy us. According to the Course, these are prayers not to God but to our **idols**.

ACIM: Asking God for the **healing** of the mind (our own or that of others) and for the **revelation** of His Presence. All prayers are answered, except when we ask for what would hurt us (*see* T-9.I.10:1), or when we are afraid to receive the answer (*see* T-9.I.1-2). We must ask in confidence, asking merely to accept what we already have. For this reason, the prayers in the Course are generally affirmative statements and never contain the word "please." The Course considers the various statements it asks us to repeat in the Workbook lessons or in the Text to be prayers. What is important is not the words of our prayers but the "prayer of the heart" (M-21.1:3). It is perfectly all right to pray to Jesus, the Holy Spirit, or the Christ. However, the Course's prayers are generally addressed to God. God does not hear our words, but our prayers in some sense do reach Him through the Holy Spirit (*see* T-15.VIII.5:5). Prayer can serve different functions:

1. "Prayer is the medium of miracles" (T-1.I.11), which means that through prayer we receive the love, the **healing**, which we extend to others in the **miracle**. We must truly ask for this healing with the prayer of our heart, and not merely with our words (*see* M-21.1-3).

2. Most of the Course's prayers ask for the healing of our own minds, ask to accept forgiveness (in some form) into our minds (*see* T-3.V.6).

3. The prayers in Part II of the Workbook are meant to be invitations to God to come and give us the experience of oneness with Him (*see* W-pII.In.3:3, 4:6).

4. In the Course itself, prayer does not occur in Heaven. However, in the *Song of Prayer* supplement, prayer occurs not only in the separated state, but in Heaven. There, it is no longer asking, but is formless communion with God, an eternal song of love (*see* **song of Heaven**) we sing to God and He sings to us (*see* S-1.In.1).

projection

The ego's distorted use of **extension**, which seems to reverse **cause and effect**. The main defense of the separation, what keeps it going (*see* T-6.II.1:5). In extension, an **idea** goes forth from our mind without leaving it, thus linking our mind to the minds we extend to. In projection, we try to throw an idea out of our mind onto a supposedly external world. This makes the idea appear to be outside us, rather than inside. Being outside, the idea now appears to be objectively real; not our own effect, but an independent cause with power over us. In this way, the pain we gave ourselves now seems given to us by others (*see* T-7.VII.8-9). Projection thus masks the very law it applies: that it is our own thoughts that cause our perceptions and experience (*see* **projection makes perception**).

1. In the **separation**, we projected our belief in separateness outward, thus making the world. A world of separation now appeared to be an objective, real cause with power over us, rather than our own illusory projection (*see* T-18.I.5-6).

2. We now use projection to try to throw outside of us our feelings of guilt. This takes the form of blaming others. Yet this simply causes more guilt, and produces a perception in which the world seems poised to take vengeance on us for our attack on it (*see* W-pI.22.1). In other words, we fear that our projections will return to our mind (*see* T-7.VIII.2-3). Projection, then, is an ego device not to rid us of guilt, but to compound guilt and increase fear.

3. The figures we see in the world, which the Course calls **dream figures**, seem to be acting independently of us and often against our interests. However, they are really animated by our own disowned thoughts, which we don't want to admit are inside of us, but prefer to see as outside of us and acting on us.

4. Projection produces our **fear of God** (along with such related beliefs as the traditional interpretation of the crucifixion; *see* T-3.I.3:8). We project onto God our belief that we are guilty, making it appear that He believes in our guilt, too, and wants to punish us for it. We think He accomplishes this through the attacks and calamities visited on us by the world (*see* W-pI.153.7:3).

"projection makes perception"

The Course's theory of perception, which is a reversal of the commonsense belief that our perception is caused from without. External objects seem to be sending information through our senses to our brains, seemingly causing our perception of them. Yet our perceptions are caused *internally*. Over time we build up beliefs about reality. These beliefs guide our *attention*, causing our eyes to search for those things that fit our pre-existing categories (M-8.4). Once we find these things, our beliefs guide our *interpretation* of them, and these interpretations *are* our perceptions (*see* T-11.VI.1-3). Our perceptions are thus projections of our beliefs, through the means of selective attention and subjective interpretation. As a result, what we see is simply a mirror, a reflection of our state of mind. *See* **perception**, **projection**. *See* T-13.V.3:5, T-21.In.1:1.

pupil

Conventional: A student who is learning under the close supervision of a teacher. Different from "student" in that one can be a student of a book, but can be a pupil only of a *teacher*.

ACIM: One who is being guided along a "way" by a teacher, whether that way is a spiritual path or a just way of living. The Course speaks of pupils of a generic teacher—one who teaches any one of the thousands of forms of the universal curriculum (*see* M-2, P-2.II). It also speaks of pupils of a teacher of *A Course in Miracles* (*see* M-17, 18, 23, 24, 29). These are newer students of the Course who are being guided along its path by a more experienced student who is in the role of mentor. In all of the above cases, a teacher is meant to pass on his particular "way" to his pupil. He does this perhaps through formal teaching, but he mostly does this through example and through the relationship itself. In this relationship, the pupil must remember that "only time divides teacher and pupil" (M-29.1:4), and that time is an illusion. This means 1) that teacher and pupil are equal in their eternal nature, 2) that the pupil has much to learn from his teacher in the particular area in which they have joined, and 3) that the pupil is there to gain equality with his teacher in that area, to become a teacher himself. *See* **teaching-learning situation**.

reality

Root meaning: What truly and permanently exists independent of deception, illusion, and subjective opinion.

Conventional: The physical world and cosmos.

ACIM: A transcendental realm known as **Heaven**, **eternity**, or the **Kingdom of God**. Reality is pure spirit. It is changeless, eternal, formless, boundless. It has no different orders or levels. It is total, one, and cannot be known partially. In it part and whole are identical; we are part of reality and all of reality. Even though reality is completely obvious, we lost awareness of it when we tried to be the author of reality, including our own reality. *See* **illusion**. *See* T-30.VIII.1, 4.

real thoughts

The thoughts we think with God, joined with His Mind. Our current thoughts are meaningless and are not actually real. They bear no relation to our real thoughts. In thinking them, we are not actually thinking. These thoughts cover over our real thoughts, which lie unchanged within the mind we share with God. In Course meditation, we sink past our unreal thoughts in order to experience our real thoughts. These thoughts will tell us that we are saved. And they will show us the **real world**. *See* **Thoughts of God**.

real world

Conventional: The world of harsh rules and hard knocks that doles out painful consequences for our mistakes and does not leave room for our naive fantasies of how things ought to be.

ACIM: The world of happiness and joy made by the Holy Spirit (*see*

T-25.III.3-5), revealed by **forgiveness**, and looked upon by **vision**, by **true perception**. The goal of the journey, the state of mind which immediately precedes the awakening to **Heaven**. An intermediate state which incorporates elements of reality and illusions (*see* T-26.III.3). Not Heaven, but a perceptual reflection of Heaven; a dream of waking. The real world is not the **world** of physical form (it has no buildings, streets, stores, day, or night; *see* T-13.VII.1) and cannot be seen with the body's eyes (*see* C-4.2:1). When we have forgiven the world, we will look out from the holiness, the Christ, within. The eyes of Christ in us will reveal an inner vision of a nonphysical realm. This realm, the real world, might be said to have two aspects:

1. It is composed of the loving thoughts that went into the making and maintaining of this world (*see* T-11.VII.2), which are all that is *real* about the *world* we made. The Holy Spirit made the real world by inspiring these loving thoughts and then by putting the rest of our thoughts through a purification process that retained *only* the love (*see* T-5.IV.8:1-6). In this state we assign a different meaning to the physical world. We interpret the same familiar physical things as symbols of loving thoughts (*see* T-17.II.5-6) rather than of fear. We see in all things nothing but the purpose of forgiveness (*see* T-30.V.1:1).

2. The real world is also composed of the **holiness** in all things, the **Son of God** in every person (*see* T-17.II.1:1-2:1). Based on this vision, we look *past* all things physical. We see physical things as mere shadows, mere illusions, and so they appear transparent as we look beyond them to the **face of Christ**.

reason

Root meaning: Sound or sane thinking. Logical thinking based on true premises, on solid reasons.

Conventional: The proper exercise of the human intellect.

ACIM: The Holy Spirit's thinking, logical thinking based on God's premises. Sane thinking by which illusions are judged as illusory and sin is reinterpreted as a mistake. The means of salvation (*see* T-22.III.3:1); the opposite of **insanity**. The ego, being insane, has no reason. It applies logic to insane premises and thus is logical but totally unreasonable. Since the conscious mind is the domain of the ego (*see* **consciousness**), left to its own devices the intellect is completely irrational (*see* T-21.V.4). Our thinking only becomes rational when it is not generated by our conscious mind, but is inspired by our **right mind**, the home of the Holy Spirit. In other words, the Holy Spirit is not arational or nonintellectual, but quite the reverse. He actually applies the rules of sound thinking far better than we do. Reason is not an ability invented by the ego and reinterpreted by the Holy Spirit, for it is fundamentally antithetical to the ego. *See* T-21.V-VI, T-22.III.

receiving

See **giving/receiving**.

response to temptation

Responding with right-minded thoughts to the **temptation** to engage in egoic thinking. According to the Course, whenever we notice any kind of upset, we should have a habit of instantly responding with a right-minded thought, especially our Workbook idea for the day. The phrase is introduced in the Text (*see* T-31.III.1:3) and used (with variations) in the Workbook. It denotes a crucial element of Course practice.

resurrection

Christian: The rising of Jesus' body, which proved that he was divine. The rising of all believers at the end of time.

ACIM:

1. The rising of the mind, and of the entire Sonship, from the ego's dream of **death** to the awareness of eternal life, from insanity to perfectly healed perception. This rising takes place due to the realization of the perfect innocence or holiness that is our true nature. This is followed by the ascension, by God taking the **final step** and lifting us into Heaven.

2. The resurrection of **Jesus**, the reawakening of his own mind (not the revivification of his body), which paved the way for his own return to knowledge (*see* T-3.V.1:3), for his own final step (*see* C-6.1:1). The resurrection was not proof of Jesus' divine status, but rather a demonstration of a general truth: that **life** cannot be destroyed, and indeed is the only reality (*see* T-3.I.7:6-7), that "there is no death" (mentioned eighteen times in the Course; *see* W-pI.163.Heading). His resurrection set in motion the **Atonement** (*see* T-3.I.1:2). In it was contained the resurrection of the entire Sonship. Thus, by identifying with it we will experience our own resurrection. Although the reappearance of Jesus' body can be seen as a symbol of the resurrection of his mind, the real resurrection was the *disappearance* of his body, not the reappearance, for that disappearance represented the removal of the limits that had been placed on the mind.

See M-28.

revelation

Root meaning: God revealing Himself to us.

Christian: God revealing to us ideas and truths, usually through the words of Scripture. ·

ACIM: God revealing **knowledge** of Himself through direct, wordless, imageless experience of union with Him (traditionally called the mystical experience). Refers both to the final or permanent experience of God in Heaven (which is the end or goal of the journey) and to temporary experiences of God while in this world (which *reveal* the end of the journey). Yet to reach this end, **miracles** are needed. They are the means and are more valuable now than revelation. *See* **grace**. *See* T-1.II.

right mind

Conventional: A state of sanity and decency that one can be in.

ACIM: A state of mind and a place in one's mind that is completely sane. The home of the Holy Spirit, **right-mindedness**, forgiveness, and miracles. It is still within the separated mind, but is the solution to the separation. This level of mind is totally unconscious, except for brief, occasional flashes. Yet the goal is to make it our normal conscious state of mind. *See* T-5.I.3:3-6.

right-mindedness

The state of mind in which salvation lies. The answer to **wrong-mindedness**, an answer which paves the way for **One-mindedness**. The state of mind the **miracle worker** must be in to extend **miracles** to others (*see* **accepting the Atonement for oneself**). "*Right-mindedness* listens to the **Holy Spirit**, **forgives** the world, and through Christ's **vision** sees the **real world** in its place" (C-1.5:2). Used only in the first four chapters of the Text and clarified in the Clarification of Terms. *See* T-2.V.3-4.

sacrifice

The act of voluntarily losing something, a) in order to gain something else, b) for the sake of a deity, c) for the sake of another person or some worthy cause.

1. Sacrifice is totally unknown to **God**, for He only gives without cost and knows nothing of loss.

2. We think, however, that God, the Holy Spirit, and Jesus ask us to sacrifice all that we hold dear, especially the things of the body. This notion severely impedes the spiritual journey, for it makes the goal seem fearful.

3. It is the ego, not God, that demands sacrifice. None of its pleasures come without the price of pain. It asks us to sacrifice totality to keep a little treasure for ourselves (*see* T-26.I). Yet this "treasure" is only loss, loneliness, and fear. Thus, the ego asks total, not partial, sacrifice. The real meaning of sacrifice, then, is "the cost of believing in illusions" (M-13.5:2).

4. Sacrifice is the basis of the **special relationship** (*see* also **giving/receiving**), where we believe that true love demands, as well as gives, sacrifice. This belief makes God's Love seem like the ultimate demand. Sacrificing for another only induces guilt, which is meant to obligate the other to sacrifice in return (*see* T-15.VII.6-9).

5. Sacrifice is an idea of our making. Only we ask sacrifice of ourselves. Yet we project this onto God and the world, thinking that their demands are the cause of our deprivation.

6. The Holy Spirit asks only the sacrifice of pain. We must give Him not sacrifice, but the whole *idea* of sacrifice.

salvation

Root meaning: Being saved from all that would hurt and limit us.

Christian: Being saved from the power and effects of sin by the atoning death of Jesus on the cross.

ACIM: Being saved from the experience of separation from God, from guilt, and from all the human ills that come from separation and guilt. Comes through the Holy Spirit's **healing** of our minds. Our **spirit** was never lost and so need not be saved. **Forgiveness** affirms this; it makes way for salvation by recognizing that who we are was never lost and that all that impedes salvation is unreal. Salvation is thus an illusion, but one that brings the end of illusions. The ego's plan for salvation is attack, which it promises will make us safe and obtain for us **idols** and **special relationships**. Yet this really brings guilt and self-punishment. The ego ascribes this punishment to God, saying that this is how He saves and that His salvation should thus be feared. In this way the ego seeks to save itself from God. *See* **Atonement, plan for salvation**. *See* W-pII.2.

savior

One who saves us with his holiness, who gives us **salvation**.

1. A minor usage is the Christ, the Holy Spirit, and Jesus.

2. The major usage is the people in our lives, especially our holy relationship partner(s). We think that our salvation comes through attacking them. Yet they are our saviors. We allow them to save us through saving *them*, through seeing their holiness with Christ's **vision**. The mere sight of their holiness saves us, and this sight will also release them to consciously and actively save us through their gratitude (*see* T-29.III.1-4). Note: Other people are our saviors because of their holiness, not because they flush our egos to the surface (though there is one reference to this; *see* W-pI.192.9).

3. Our **function**, then, is to be a savior to others, which we do by seeing salvation in them, by seeing them as *our* saviors.

4. The ego sees death, fear, specialness, and the body as our saviors. *See* **witness**. *See* T-20.II.9-11.

script

Seldom used in the Course, this term occurs in only one Text section (T-30.VII)—definition #1 below—and in two related Workbook lessons

(158 and 169)—definition #2 below.

1. Our "plans for what the day *should* be" (T-30.VII.2:1). In this script (which we are constantly changing), we assign everyone and everything a role for that day. How well they play their role in our script determines, in our eyes, whether the day was a success or failure.

2. The script of our passage through time and space. This script has set the part we are to play, every step we take along the way, and the time of our final awakening. This script *is* followed, because it has all already happened. Now, instead of actually living it for the first time, we are merely "reviewing mentally what has gone by" (W-pI.158.4:5). This script was written by the Holy Spirit ("Him Who wrote salvation's script in His Creator's Name"—W-pI.169.9:3), but also incorporates decisions of our own (*see* W-pI.169.8:2).

Second Coming

Christian: The bodily return of **Jesus** on the last day to judge the world.

ACIM: The collective return of our awareness of the **Christ**, our true Identity. A time in which all minds are freed of the ego's rule. The First Coming of Christ was God's creation of our true Self; the Second Coming is the return of our awareness of our true Self. It ends the Holy Spirit's lessons and allows all minds to hear the Holy Spirit's judgment, which is the basis for what comes after it: the **Last Judgment** (*see* W-pII.10.1:1-2). Though it is not the return of Jesus, he is in charge of it. *See* T-4.IV.10, T-9.IV.9, W-pII.9.

self

1. When capitalized, refers to the **Christ**, the true Identity of ourselves and all living things (*see* W-pII.6).

2. In lowercase, generally refers to the **ego**, the self we *think* we are, the false self we invented. This self was made, not created, is enormously variable and unstable, and is in total opposition to God.

self-concept

The concept we form of our self (also called "the concept of the self"). We spend our growing-up years trying to fashion a self-concept that fits the world and can meet its demands. But this concept is not an attempt to mirror who we really are, for our reality cannot be conceptualized or imaged. We are not an image. The self-image we make, then, is like a graven image; it is an idol designed to replace our divinity, our true **Self**. Our self-concept holds that we are weak, lacking, victimized, guilty, and primarily physical. This self-concept needs to be replaced. We do so by giving our brother a concept of himself as forgiven, innocent, and worthy of our faith. This will then become our concept of ourselves. And this more beneficent self-concept will pave the way for us to awaken from all self-concepts and discover Who we really are. *See* T-31.V.

separation, the

The event in which we apparently separated from God, which gave birth to the entire phenomenal universe, including form, **time**, space, and perception, and which the mind re-enacts in nearly every instant. The apparent split with God for which the **Atonement** is the reconciliation or remedy. The "detour into fear" (T-2.I.2:1); the "descent from magnitude into littleness" (T-10.IV.8:5); "the denial of union" (T-12.I.10:6). The separation began with the idea that we could make ourselves into separate beings who were both **special** in the eyes of their Creator (*see* T-13.III.10:2) and were self-created (*see* T-10.V.4:3, T-21.II.10). This produced what seemed to be a real event in which we tore ourselves out of God's Mind (*see* T-5.V.3), shattered Heaven into countless separate bodies and intervals of time (*see* T-28.III.7:4), became isolated entities, and then made a world of separate individuals, forms, and moments. Yet the separation was merely a psychological event, in which, through denial and **dissociation**, we fell asleep to reality and dreamt of separation (*see* **sleep**). In our **dream**, this experience has lasted billions of years, but in reality it lasted only an instant, for God's Answer ended it immediately. And even this instant never occurred (*see* M-2.2:8). The core message of the Course is that *"the separation never occurred"* (T-6.II.10:7).

shadow figures

Dark mental images/memories of particular people from our past who did not fulfill the roles we assigned to them, who did not give us the special love that we wanted from them. We try to replay our past with them in the present and this time turn the tables—take vengeance on them and get from them the love we wanted. We do this by forming **special relationships** with people who remind us of our shadow figures. We try to extract from these new people what the shadow figures did not give us, what we think they stole from us. In the present, then, we are really interacting with memories, not with our current partners. *See* T-13.IV.6, T-13.V.2-6, T-17.III.1-3, T-29.IV.5:6.

sickness

1. Sickness is of the mind. It is **insanity**, mental illness, **wrong-mindedness**, the condition of the mind that believes in **separation**.

2. Physical sickness is made by us, by projecting onto the body our mental sickness. This projection is for a purpose: It reinforces the supposed "reality" of the ego. The Course mentions many ways in which sickness serves this purpose: a) The mind punishes the body to mitigate expected punishment from God and so usurp His perceived function (*see* T-5.V.5:4-9); b) the mind makes the body sick to prove that it is stronger than God Who would heal (*see* M-5.I.1-2); c) the mind punishes the body as a way of blaming the body for the "sins" the mind had the body act out (*see* T-18.VI.6:1); d) the mind punishes the body as a way of punishing itself for its supposed sins; e) the mind made the body out of the sickness of separation and projects this sickness onto the body (*see* T-19.I.7:7); f) the mind uses sickness to demonstrate that the mind is separate from goodness, health, and God (*see* T-28.V.1:1-5); g) the mind produces sickness to separate us from others (*see* W-pI.137.1-2); h) the mind makes the body sick to show how another has injured it (*see* T-27.I.3-4); i) the mind attacks the body because the body has failed to satisfy (*see* T-19.IV(B).11:6); j) the mind attacks the body to prove that the body is real (*see* T-29.II.8:1-3), that we are physical beings, not spiritual (*see* W-pI.136.7-8); k) the mind attacks the body because it suspects the body is not real enough to truly act out the mind's fantasies (*see* T-18.VI.3:7); l) the mind makes the body sick to hide the fact that the real problem is in the mind, that the mind "attacks itself and wants to die" (W-pI.76.5:5).

3. The one true remedy for sickness is not physical medicine (though this can be appropriate to use; *see* **magic**), but the **miracle**, which heals all sickness regardless of form, thus proving that sickness is an **illusion** (*see* W-pI.140).

sin

The violation of the laws of God or goodness. A real **attack** that causes real damage, violation, and injury, produces real moral and spiritual **guilt**, and calls for punishment and **death**. "To sin would be to violate reality, and to succeed. Sin is the proclamation that attack is real and guilt is justified" (*see* T-19.II.2:2-3). Also, the *state* of separation and inner corruption that results from the *act* of sin (*see* T-30.III.3:7).

1. Sin is the ego's foundation and most holy idea (*see* T-19.II.5). The archetypal sin was the **separation**. The ego sees sin as a power beyond God's that attacked and overthrew His Will and wrenched His creation away from Him, shattering its oneness and corrupting its innocence (*see* T-19.III.8:1-3). The ego's *goal* is to make this a permanent, eternal reality.

2. Sin is the basis for the ego's perception of the world. It sees sin everywhere and in everyone. This perception is the source of **anger** and **fear**.

3. The Holy Spirit knows that sin is an **illusion**, a belief in something that can never occur (in fact, the word "sin" in the Course is often shorthand for the erroneous "belief in sin"). For God's laws cannot be violated, attack and injury are unreal, guilt and death are impossible, and the separation from God never occurred. What we call sin is merely an **error**, a mistake. This means it can be corrected and calls only for correction, not punishment (*see* **call for love/help**). This is the basis for **forgiveness**.

See T-19.II-III, W-pII.4.

sleep

Conventional: A state of unawareness and forgetfulness in which the mind withdraws from "reality" into a private state and dreams of senseless things that are not real.

ACIM: A state of unawareness and forgetfulness in which the mind elects to withdraw from true **reality** into a private state of **insanity**, where it **dreams** of being in another place (besides **Heaven**), another time (besides **eternity**) and even of being another person (besides the **Son of God**). This state is not truly real, however, for "God creates only mind awake" (*see* W-pI.167.8:1).

something else

Refers to a false alternative we have invented in order to get away from the truth. Usually refers to something we have chosen in preference to **reality** or the Kingdom of God; especially the thing we wish to be (the ego) in place of our true Identity (*see* T-22.I.3:5-6, 7:4, 8:5, 10:4). Also refers to the things we think are causing us pain (e.g., outer attacks), but which are displacements of the real problem—our own unforgiveness (*see* T-27.VII.1:4).

song of Heaven

The joyous hymn of love and gratitude that all creation sings in praise of God (*see* T-26.IV.3:5), and that God sings in praise of us (*see* T-24.II.4:4-5). The song of creating. This still, formless song is the condition of Heaven (*see* W-pI.183.11) and is characterized by gratitude. Called "the song of prayer" in the *Song of Prayer* supplement. This song is reflected and anticipated in salvation's song, in which the Sonship joyously sings its thankfulness to Heaven for saving us from the ego. *See* T-21.I.6-7.

Son of God

Christian: Jesus, who, as God's Son, is seen to have a uniquely intimate relationship with God in which nothing of God's is held back from him.

ACIM: The true Identity of every living thing; Who we really are. This term is meant as a correction of the traditional meaning of "Son of God" (thus replacing it with "Daughter of God" or "Child of God" would defeat its teaching purpose). The Course has transformed this from an exclusive term that refers only to Jesus to an inclusive one that denotes a single universal Self Who encompasses all beings, male and female (*see* **he, him**), human and nonhuman, and Whose relationship with God is compared to the perfect father-son relationship. A son is an extension, a continuation, of his father, who completes his father and is his father's joy. Therefore he receives his father's name and all of his father's love, inherits all that his father has, and is like his father in all ways. As God's extension, we complete Him and are His treasure, His joy. We receive all of His Love, all that He has, all of Himself. We receive His Name, His Identity, and are like Him in all ways. In return,

He is our Father, our Source, our one devotion and only Love. The Son of God is a fairly elastic term and can be used in several different ways:

1. The **Christ**, the collective Self of all Sons of God (used with an uppercase "He").

2. An "individual" Son of God, either asleep and apparently separated or (more rarely) awake in Heaven (lowercase "he"). There are an infinite number of these "individual" parts; hence, the frequent term "Sons of God."

3. Occasionally refers to the **Sonship**, the collectivity of all the sleeping Sons (lowercase "he").

See **God**.

Sonship

The sum of all that God created; all the parts of the **Son of God**; the collectivity which includes the minds of all **living things**. The Sonship is a plural term, indicating some kind of plurality in Heaven, yet the Sonship is perfectly united in its one Self, the **Christ**.

soul

Conventional: A spiritual element in humans that is individual and is from God, yet which can fall from grace, become corrupted and ensnared in what is not of God, and finally either become lost or become purified, perfected, and return to God.

ACIM: The term "soul" occurred frequently in the original dictation of the first eleven chapters of the Text, after which it appeared in only two passages (T-12.VI.1 and C-1.3:2). Before the Course was published, nearly all of the early references to soul were edited out or changed to other terms, primarily "spirit" and "mind." The references that remain either refer to what people believe about the soul (T-4.II.9:5-6) or allude to biblical passages that mention the soul (T-5.II.7, T-12.VI.1). A passage in the Clarification of Terms explains, "The term 'soul' is not used except in direct biblical quotations because of its highly controversial nature. It would, however, be an equivalent of 'spirit,' with the understanding that, being of God, it is eternal and was never born" (C-1.3:2-3). In the original dictation, the term referred not to spirit in general, but to *one's own spirit*, that element in each person that is of God, is perfect, changeless, and eternal. *See* **spirit**.

spark

1. The little spark. A light, placed in us by God at our creation, which sparks the **Great Rays**, which lights the lamp from which they shine. In the separated condition, the Rays are obscure, but the spark has been kept alive by God (*see* T-10.IV.7:5-8:7). Seeing the spark in others is the way to heal them, and will reveal to us the Great Rays. The spark in our own minds is the means by which we see the ego as meaningless (*see* T-11.In.3:6). Welcoming the Holy Spirit into our minds will allow this spark to expand (into the Great Rays) and sweep us out of darkness and into God (*see* T-11.II.5-6).

2. The spark of beauty (closely related to the little spark). The small amount of love that went into the making of our relationships in this world; the loving thoughts from the past. Through focusing on these and forgiving the rest, we will see the spark and let it transform our relationships into beauty (*see* T-17.III.5-7).

special function

The special form given to each individual of the one **function** of extending forgiveness (*see* **extension**), of being a **savior**. The function we gave ourselves was **specialness**, which is achieved by attacking and diminishing our brother, and which we chose in order to hurt ourselves. The **Holy Spirit**, however, translated our desire for specialness into our special function, our special part or role in His **plan for salvation**. It reverses specialness. It is our special way of serving and exalting all our brothers, rather than trying to put them beneath us so that we feel superior. The Holy Spirit gives us a special form of extending healing which is suited to our particular strengths (*see* W-pI.154.2:2). He also sends us particular people whom it is our function to save. This seems to begin with one person, our **holy relationship** partner (*see* T-20.IV.5:3). Then we and our partner are given a joint special function, which includes particular people to save. Ultimately, the ones we are appointed to save include everyone (*see* T-31.VII.10:5). The Holy Spirit also gives us guidance and supply for every aspect of this function as well as the strength to carry it out. This is our part in the fulfillment of the Holy Spirit's own special function (*see* **function**, #3). *See* T-25.VI.

specialness

The idea of being set apart from others *and* set above others. Having more or being more than others. Specialness is the great payoff promised by the ego. Our attempt to gain special favor from God was the "tiny, mad desire" (T-25.I.5:5) that sparked the **separation**, that was the root of **sin** (*see* T-24.II.3:1-3), and that set us in opposition to the Will of God (for He knows no specialness). No price is too dear for us to pay for obtaining specialness. We seek it in our **special relationships**, where others give us special love and their special selves. In this way we try to symbolically extract from them the specialness that God denied us (*see* T-16.V). We seek it with our **body**, adorning our body in order to attract it. We also seek it by accumulating **idols** (*see* T-29.VIII.8). All ways of seeking it involve **attack**, for specialness requires that others must be beneath us. It causes us to look for and rejoice at any sin we see in others. It makes everyone our enemy and so makes us feel attacked from every quarter. Because specialness is a form of separateness, it makes us feel weak, frail, isolated, and alone. And because it is a form of attack, it makes us feel guilty and afraid. *See* T-24.

special relationships

A relationship based on the pursuit of **specialness**, in which we try to a) have a special arrangement (an exclusive relationship) with and b) receive special treatment from c) a very special person, so that d) we can feel more special. Can exist between lovers, friends, or any nonenemies, though the Course discussions seem to primarily have romance in mind. The term "special relationship" is a *synonym* for "special love relationship" (there is only one fleeting reference to "special hate relationship"—*see* T-16.IV.1:1—and the idea is not a part of the concept of special relationship). The ego's system naturally produces a hostile, painful relationship with the world, which deprives us of the love we want. To keep our allegiance, the ego must provide something that offers a semblance of the love we really want, yet still is of the ego. This is the special relationship, "the ego's most boasted gift" (T-16.V.3:1). It seems to be a Heaven on earth, a haven of love in a world of hate, our greatest hope of **happiness** in a world of pain (*see* T-16.IV.3). Yet it is an illusion of **love**, a love that is unlike God's, for He knows no special love. It is a disguise, a *form* (or an appearance) of love that covers a *content* of hate and attack (*see* T-17.IV.8-9), a content exactly like the rest of the ego's system, which results in the same separateness, guilt, and fear. We can describe the relationship in stages:

1. First we search for a person different from the rest, one who is more special and has a special **body** with special parts (*see* T-15.V.2-3). Yet this process separates that person from her wholeness, for she *is* the whole. It reduces her from infinite magnitude down to a little pile of body parts (*see* T-15.V.7).

2. Then we offer her special behaviors and gifts that give her our specialness and, ultimately, give her our "self" (*see* T-16.V.7-8). These "gifts," however, are attacks designed to make her guilty and so induce her to give her "self" in return (*see* **giving/receiving**).

3. We (almost certainly) do not receive from her the specialness we think we paid for. So we resort increasingly to taking vengeance on her for not reciprocating (*see* T-16.V.1). Whether we break up or stick it out, we almost inevitably feel disillusioned (*see* T-16.IV.4). There is truth in this response, for the love *was* an illusion.

4. The Holy Spirit, however, would not deprive us of these relationships (*see* T-17.IV.2:3) or have us throw them away. He would transform them into **holy relationships**, through **forgiveness** and the **holy instant**. Yet most holy relationships are still special relationships (*see* T-18.V.5:2-3). They are holy relationships-in-training; they have accepted the goal of holiness but have not yet reached that goal. Also called the "unholy relationship" in Chapters 17-22.

See **shadow figures**. *See* T-15.V, VII, T-16.IV-VII, T-17.III-IV.

spirit

The substance of which God created His Son, of our true nature. Spirit is completely nonphysical, formless, changeless, holy, and perfect. It has only **knowledge** and no **perception**. It cannot descend into error and is unaware of the ego. It uses the mind to express itself in this world, so that the **mind** can be restored to spirit. *See* **level confusion**. *See* W-pI.97.

split mind

A **mind** divided against itself, in which the more conscious half of the mind is walled off from its own true nature by denial, fear, and dissociation. This split, which is apparent but not real, is then projected outward and symbolized by a split between the mind and other minds (*see* T-12.III.7). In this divided state, the mind cannot truly create or communicate, for what it produces is ambivalent and contradictory.

1. The primary split is between the separated mind and its real Identity, the Christ Mind.

2. The secondary split is within the separated mind, between the **ego** and the **Holy Spirit**. The Holy Spirit is the Guide out of the split, for He is a unified Presence in the mind (*see* T-25.I.7:2-3).

substitute

To replace a thing with something else. The separation began when the ego substituted its will for God's Will, illusion for reality, fear for **love**. This ancient substitution is reflected now in our **special relationships**, in which we substitute one person for another. We do not realize just how alien this is to God, Who never chooses one person in place of another. In all our relationships, we seek not love, but rather the magical substitute for love (*see* T-23.II.12). However, the substitute for love is war, and that is exactly what we find. In the end, our substitutes never satisfy, for, quite simply, "there is no substitute for Heaven" (W-pI.182.3:6; the phrase "there is no substitute" occurs five times in the Course). Our substitutes not only do not satisfy, they have no reality, for we cannot truly replace what God created. We must acknowledge this, and follow the Holy Spirit as He seeks to reverse our substitution process. He would substitute forgiveness for our condemnation, the real world for our world, Christ's vision for our perception, and the realization of our true Self for our self-concept. Yet on the road back, we must be careful not substitute the Holy Spirit's gifts with the ego's replacements for them, for that would merely be to repeat the original substitution "that shattered Heaven" (T-18.I.12:2).

teacher of God

One whose function is to teach others on behalf of God; a bringer of salvation, a **savior**, a **miracle worker**. This term is used only in the Manual for Teachers, which is written for experienced students of the Course who are ready to take on their **special function**. The Manual mentions two forms that this **function** may take. One is that of a healer, who goes to physically ill patients to extend the **healing** power of the **miracle**. The other is that of a spiritual teacher, who joins with **pupils** and teaches them his path of awakening. The following process of development is described:

1. A beginning teacher of God is one who has made one deliberate choice in which he saw someone else's interests as the same as his (*see* M-1.1). His pupils then are drawn to him and join with him in the common goal of learning the same spiritual path (*see* M-2).

2. Through these holy relationships he becomes an *advanced teacher of God* who acquires the ten characteristics of God's teachers (*see* M-4).

3. He finally transcends the world and becomes a *Teacher of teachers* (*see* M-26.2). From his position beyond the body he now will guide and inspire those teachers who are still in the body, working through them to save the world.

See **extension, teaching**.

teaching

Conventional: Imparting to others intellectual facts or concepts. This is done primarily through words and is a special activity in which one engages only a small portion of one's time.

ACIM: The extension of one's fundamental **thought system** (either the ego's or the Holy Spirit's) to others. This is done not so much by the *form* of our communication, but by the *content* we are communicating. Thus it is done primarily by example or demonstration. And it is done all the time; we cannot help but teach. Our **special function** is to extend right-minded ideas (e.g., **forgiveness**) to others. In this sense, teaching is synonymous with **healing**. As we see these ideas go forth from us and heal others, our belief in them becomes strengthened (*see* **giving/receiving**). Teaching, then, is the way in which we truly learn (*see* **learning**); thus the phrase "As you teach so shall you learn" (T-5.IV.6:4). *See* **extension**, **teacher of God**. *See* M-In.

teaching-learning situation

The Course's term (used only in M-2, M-3, and M-4) for a teacher-pupil relationship, which is a *situation* in which a teacher is *teaching* and a pupil is *learning*. This situation need not be formal—our most important teachers are often simply people we respect and whose example we follow. It need not be overtly spiritual—the Course mentions two students walking home together and becoming friends (M-3.2). And it need not be long-term—it can be a brief encounter on an elevator (M-3.2). But the ultimate goal of each teaching-learning situation is for it to become a **holy relationship**, in which teacher and pupil join in a single goal and gradually learn to overlook all the differences between them and see the face of Christ in each other. When this holy relationship is achieved, both are bumped ahead immeasurably on their journey. The pupil becomes a teacher of God and the teacher becomes an advanced teacher. *See* **pupil** and **teacher of God**.

temptation

The inner pull to engage in egoic thinking or behavior. This temptation seems to be an involuntary pull towards some forbidden pleasure, which has an unfortunate after-effect of guilt. Yet it is really a voluntary *wish*, a wish *for* guilt, hell, and misery (*see* T-31.VII.10:1). We must learn, however, that temptation is simply "another chance to choose again" (T-31.VIII.4:2), through **response to temptation**.

things

Usually used generically, but sometimes refers specifically to concrete, physical things (as in T-13.VII.1, 10, 12 and W-pII.346.1).

Thoughts of God

Thoughts as we know them are private, fleeting products of an individual mind. Yet these are not **real thoughts**. In contrast, Thoughts of God are eternal, formless realities, without birth or death, beginning or end. They are not private, but infinitely shared. They are not pictures of reality but are **reality** itself. We, His Sons, are Thoughts of God. *See* T-30.III.7-8.

thought system

An interrelated system of **ideas** that is centered on a view of who you are, provides a picture of reality and your relationship with it, and provides goals and how to attain them. You use your thought system to organize your reality. It is the basis for your thoughts, emotions, perceptions, and behaviors. There are only two thought systems, the ego's and God's (or the Holy Spirit's, which is a reflection of God's). Each one is internally consistent, yet they are diametrically opposed in foundation, in nature, and in result. You cannot reconcile them by combining them or vacillating between them. You must choose all of one and none of the other. The Course treats its own thought system as a version of the Holy Spirit's and claims its thought system is consistent, complete (*see* W-pI.42.7:2), cohesive, and includes no fear. *See* T-11.In.1.

time

The linear progression of separate moments that is the context for change, attack, birth, and death.

1. There is no time in **reality**, in **eternity**, and thus time is an **illusion**.

2. Time resulted from our apparent shattering of the one moment of eternity in the **separation**. Time's separate moments are really only a single moment, a fragment of eternity seen as non-eternal and as multiple. All of time, and the long journey it contains, took only a tiny instant in eternity (*see* T-26.V.3) before it was answered by God and was ended (*see* **Holy Spirit**). We are now at the end of time looking back on it, mentally reviewing it like we would a past conversation or movie (*see*

M-2.2-4). We cannot change the basic progression of our movie (since it already happened), but we can "fast forward" through parts of it by accepting **miracles** (*see* T-1.II.6).

3. The ego tries to make time last forever by seeking to endlessly repeat the past. It tells us to take revenge for past injustices. Yet this is really a trick to get us to repeat *past* sins and so reinforce *present* **guilt** and fear of *future* punishment.

4. The Holy Spirit places all His focus on now, on undoing the past by releasing others from it (*see* **forgiveness**) and entering the present moment (*see* **holy instant**), the only moment that is real and the only moment in which we can change our minds. In the present moment we can experience eternity, since the present is a shard of eternity (*see* T-17.IV.11, 15). From this present moment a new future can extend, which does not repeat the past and which will lead us back to eternity. This is the only purpose of time.

treasure house

Also called the "treasury," "store," "storehouse," and "storehouse of treasures." The deep place in our mind that holds all the treasures that God has stored up for us. This treasure house contains a limitless supply. Its doors are always open wide in welcome, and its gifts are freely available just for the asking. The treasures are not gold and silver but **miracles**. We must open the storehouse of our mind, receive its miracles, and give them away (W-pI.159.2:5). When we take from its treasures, the store does not diminish, but actually increases. Our ultimate goal is to invite everyone into our treasure house (which is their treasure house, too) and have them join us in a joyous feast of miracles, in which there is no lack and no end, and where God and Christ will join us (*see* T-28.III.7-9).

true perception

The goal of the Course; **salvation**. Usually called "vision" or "Christ's vision"; called "spiritual sight" early in the Text. The sight which comes out of the state of **right-mindedness** and looks upon the **real world**. True perception is the opposite of false or conventional **perception**. False perception sees the **projection** of our insane illusions. It sees a world of **sin**, of forms, changes, and differences. It condemns what it looks on and separates from it in fear. True perception, on the other hand, sees everything as it truly is: perfect. It sees only sinlessness, innocence, **holiness** (*see* W-pI.158.7), seeing always the same maximal light of Christ in everything (*see* **face of Christ**). It forgives all it sees, blessing it with **miracles** and joining with it in love. True perception does not function like conventional perception. Rather than seeing through our body's eyes (*see* C-4.2:1), it sees through the **eyes of Christ** in us (and thus operates irrespective of distance or changes in lighting). Rather than seeing bodies, it sees holiness. Rather than using the brain to interpret sense data, it is born as a pure "knowing" straight from the Christ in us (*see* T-22.I.2). Rather than seeing visual images, it sees pure content, pure meaning (as when a sudden recognition prompts one to say, "I see"; *see* T-22.III.1:4-7). It may, however, be symbolized and preceded by the seeing of light around visual objects (*see* W-pI.15.2-3). From the perspective of true perception, all that our eyes now see will be reinterpreted. We will experience forms as unreal, as transparent (*see* W-pI.159.5), and will mentally look past them to the light of holiness. We will see all forms as having the same purpose: forgiveness. And we will let the Holy Spirit interpret people's behavior for us, focusing on the loving behavior and interpreting all other behavior as a **call for love**. True perception is our natural sight and is available to us whenever we want it. If it is achieved with respect to anything, it will transfer to everything. However, one exception will block its transfer (*see* W+pI.In.5). When true perception is complete, God will take the **final step** and carry us over into **knowledge**.

truth

Root meaning: What is true, real, fact; the opposite of illusion.

ACIM: Transcendental **reality** or **Heaven**, beyond time and space, including all **ideas** inherent in reality. Only that is true, real, only that is Fact. All else is **illusion**. Truth was created by God. It is total, indivisible, all-inclusive, constant, changeless. It cannot be destroyed and when attacked it does not respond. It cannot be perceived, learned, nor believed. It can only be known (*see* **knowledge**). It is given; truth is not up to you to establish. Truth is only joy and safety. The truth about you is grandeur, perfection. Yet you have feared truth and denied it (*see* **denial**), making illusions instead. Truth and illusions are mutually exclusive. To discover truth you must search out all that interferes with it (*see* T-14.VII.2:1). You must learn to distinguish between truth and illusion, letting illusions go without exception. Then "truth will dawn upon you of itself" (T-8.VI.9:11). *See* **bringing darkness to light, illusions to truth**. *See* W-pI.152.2-5.

unhealed healer

One who tries to heal without **accepting the Atonement for oneself**; the ego's version of the true **miracle worker**. "By definition, he is trying to give what he has not received [e.g., healing]" (T-9.V.1:4). The unhealed healer does not believe there is **no order of difficulty in miracles,** and so finds many things too difficult to heal (*see* T-5.VII.2). He makes sin and sickness real, and then tries to dispel them. He does not know how to give, and instead wants to get (gratitude and money) from his patients. He thinks he is in charge of the healing situation. The Course specifically mentions two examples of unhealed healer (*see* T-9.V).

1. The unhealed psychotherapist, who looks into his patient's dreams and hidden thoughts to uncover who the patient really is. Since these come from the patient's ego, they reveal the patient to be an attacking ego. The patient already believes this and feels guilty for it, and so the therapist grants her a kind of forgiveness by telling her that her attacking thoughts will not have any effect if she does not act them out.

2. The unhealed theologian, who believes in the reality of sin in himself and who fears God's punishment. He therefore believes in the sinfulness of those who come to him, but tells them that their sins can be magically wiped away by the forgiveness of a distant God.

See T-7.V.7. *See* also the *Psychotherapy* supplement, P-2.VII.4-7, P-3.III.2:1.

universe

Conventional: The totality of physical existence, which includes stars, planets, and galaxies.

ACIM: The totality of true existence, true **reality**, which was created by God and is "beyond the sun and stars" (M-20.6:11), "beyond the petty sum of all the separate bodies you perceive" (T-15.VIII.4:5). It is a virtual synonym for God's **creation**, the sum total of what He created, in that it can refer to the **Sonship** in its heavenly state *or* in its separated state.

veil

1. Anything that blocks our awareness of reality, or our awareness of the real world. The Course mentions the veil of time, of guilt, of fantasies. Veils seem dark and heavy but are thin and easily lifted by our desire to see past them.

2. Specifically, the veil across the **face of Christ** (the image here is of a facial veil). This veil is the **fear of God**, the final obstacle to peace. It is also said to be specialness, idols, the **attraction of guilt** and death, the **gap** between us and our brother. We reach the place before the veil by joining with our holy relationship partner. In order to look on the veil without terror, we must first be willing to look on our partner with forgiveness. Then together we will lift the veil and look on the face of Christ. Then we will rise in **resurrection** past the veil and disappear into the Presence beyond the veil: God. *See* T-19.IV(D).

vigilance

The mental stance of being constantly alert and watchful, especially for threat. Vigilance only occurs within the **split mind**, in which each half is a threat to the other.

1. "The ego exerts maximal vigilance about what it permits into awareness" (T-4.V.1:3). Now we currently exercise vigilance on the ego's behalf.

2. The Holy Spirit also exerts maximal vigilance, and we must learn to be vigilant on His behalf. We must learn to be alert to all **temptation** to think with the ego (*see* **response to temptation**) and to allow into our minds only what God put there. Then we will go beyond the split mind and thus beyond vigilance. *See* T-6.V(C), T-7.VI.

vision
  See **true perception**.

Voice for God, God's Voice
  See the **Holy Spirit**.

way

Often used in the generic sense of "manner," "fashion," or "method." But often used to mean a path or course along which one travels to a destination. In this sense, it can refer to the ego's way, which leads nowhere, but most often refers to the Holy Spirit's way, which leads to God. For instance, "Love is the way I walk in gratitude" (W-pI.195.Heading) does not mean "Love is the manner in which I walk." Instead, it means "Love is the pathway I walk, and I do so in gratitude."

will

Conventional: One's desire or intention; what one wants or intends to happen. The mental faculty by which one sets in motion what one wants to happen.

ACIM: The faculty by which one creates or extends in Heaven (*see* **creation** and **extension**). Will is undivided. It requires a whole, united mind with absolutely no ambivalence or uncertainty. Strictly speaking, will exists only in Heaven. The **split mind** is inherently divided and thus is incapable of willing or creating. It can only wish or **make** or choose (*see* **choice**). *See* **Will of God**.

Will of God

Root meaning: What God "wants" and has ordained; the instrument of God's expression and creation.

Conventional: Generally refers to God's plan for our lives, which often includes sacrifice. Thus it is used to explain all those things that are painful, tragic, and hard to understand, but must be accepted because they are God's Will.

ACIM: God wills only Heaven, only unlimited love and **happiness** without end (*see* **creation**). God's Will is limitless, changeless power that can never be opposed. It is not gradual in accomplishment but creates instantaneous and eternal Fact.

1. In Heaven, you were created by God's Will and *are* God's Will—the extension of His Mind, Spirit, and Self. His Will for you is perfect happiness, eternal oneness with Him and with your brothers.

2. On earth, you believe that your will and God's Will are in opposition. This is because you have identified with an alien will, for His Will and your true will are one and the same. You *are* His Will. Fearing His Will thus means fearing your own will and your own reality. Since His Will is *not* an alien will, it cannot be forced upon you but must be freely welcomed.

3. God's Will for you on earth is contained in His **plan for salvation** (*see* W-pI.100:2-4).

witness

Something which points to the truth of something else. Primary meaning: the effect of a cause, the existence of which points to the reality of the cause (*see* **cause and effect**).

1. In Heaven, you are the witness to your Cause, God, establishing Him as Father and Creator (*see* T-13.VIII.9:2).

2. In Heaven, your creations are witness to your own fatherhood (*see* T-9.VI.5:5).

3. On earth, all perceptions witness to the **thought system**, the state of mind, that caused them (*see* T-21.In.1:1-5).

4. The ego uses physical and emotional evidence, such as fear and physical illness, to witness to its own supposed reality (*see* T-8.VIII.3:5-4:9).

5. The miracles you do bear witness to the power of the Holy Spirit within you (*see* T-14.X.6:10).

6. Those whom you heal become witnesses to the healing, the holiness, in you, and so become your **saviors** (*see* T-13.VI.9:2).

7. Those whom you attack bear witness to the ego in you.

8. Your health and **invulnerability** witness to the innocence in your brother, to the fact that his sin had no effect on you and so was not a cause.

Word of God

Christian: Often used to refer to the Bible or to Jesus as the *Logos*.

ACIM: The message of salvation that God speaks to us through His Voice (the Holy Spirit) in answer to the separation, by which the separation disappears. Sometimes characterized as a promise God makes to us that we will find salvation in the end (*see* W-pII.355.1:2). Sometimes the Word by which God created His Son (*see* W-pII.276.1:1-3). The one unified Word from which come all the Holy Spirit's specific words, teaching, and guidance (*see* W-pI.198.6). Basically synonymous with the **Atonement**, **forgiveness**, and God's **plan for salvation**. This "Word" is not a verbal word, but it is a kind of symbol, which stands for the changelessness of God's Love. Verbal approximations would thus include "**I am as God created me**" and "My Son is pure and holy as Myself" (W-pII.276.1:2). It is our **function** to speak this Word to the world, to let this Word guide our words so that they become human symbols of God's Word (*see* M-21.5). When we clear away the words we have written on the world (the meanings we have ascribed to it) we will see only God's Word written on it, transforming it into a symbol of Heaven (*see* W-pI.192.4:1). This is the final perception in which all symbols vanish. Does not refer to the Bible, nor Jesus, nor the Course (though these may in fact reflect the Word of God). *See* W-pI.125.

world

1. The physical earth and entire physical realm, which is an **illusion**. A realm of **time**, in which all things change and have a beginning and an end. A realm of space, in which all things are separate and lonely, trapped in bodies. A realm of **fear**, in which all things are under constant attack. A realm of pain, because everything attacks and nothing satisfies. A realm of **insanity**, governed by the "**laws**" of chaos (*see* T-23.II). A realm of **death**, in which all things must die. God did not create the world (*see* W-pI.152.6-7), for it is literally Heaven's diametric opposite (*see* T-16.V.3:6) in which everything is upside down and backwards from reality (*see* T-18.I.5-6). It is not our home, for it is not our place of origin, it does not shelter us and we do not belong here. Instead of God creating the world, *we* made the world as an opposite to Him, a place His Love and Oneness could enter not (*see* W-pII.3.2:1-4), a way of proving the **Will of God** has been overthrown. It is our **projection**, which seems to prove that separation, sin, and fear are objective realities thrust on us from without, rather than subjective ideas that we can let go at any time. It is our **dream**, which was dreamt out of the idea of **sin**, out of the lesson that "God's Son is guilty" (T-31.I.7:4; *see* "**God's Son is guiltless**"). As such, the very nature of the world is to constantly punish us for our supposed sinfulness and guilt, attacking us with pain, **sickness**, and **death** (*see* T-13.In.2-4). This "proves" that fear is real (and fear is the essence of the ego). And it "proves" that **fear of God** is justified, for we assume that God made this world of fear and death. The world has no objective existence: "There is no world!" (W-pI.132.6:2). It is merely a set of **ideas** inside our sleeping minds in Heaven. The world will disappear when we let this set of ideas go (*see* M-14). Rather than trying to change the world to suit our wishes, we must choose to see the world differently. The Holy Spirit sees it as a teaching device for bringing us home (*see* T-5.III.11:1), as "a place where the Son of God finds his freedom" (W-pI.rI.57.3:6), as a place whose only purpose is forgiveness (*see* M-14.2:1-6). He teaches us to see the **real world**.

2. The global community of minds that are asleep, need saving, and will eventually return to Heaven. It is important to distinguish between this sense of "world" and the preceding one. When the Course says, "I was persecuted as the world judges" (T-6.I.5:3), it does not mean "as the mountains and trees judge"; it means as the human race judges. Likewise, when the Course says, "Our true purpose is to save the world" (W-pI.153.8:2), it does not mean saving the forms of the world, but rather saving the *minds*.

See T-18.IX.3-4, T-25.VII.4, W-pI.132.

wrong-mindedness

The opposite of **right-mindedness**, the state of mind based on the ego's **thought system**, which is the source of false perception (*see* description in **true perception**) and of all human ills. "*Wrong-mindedness* listens to the ego and makes illusions; perceiving sin and justifying anger, and seeing guilt, disease and death as real" (C-1.6:1). Used only in the first four chapters of the Text and clarified in the Clarification of Terms.

you

The person the Course addresses itself to. A sleeping **Son of God**, who remains in Heaven, part of the Christ and at one with God, yet who **dreams** that he is an ego, a frail, sinful human being living in a body in the world of space and time. The tiny part of your total identity that is asleep and needs redemption, that has a separated or **split mind**, that thinks private thoughts, experiences painful emotions, and can choose (*see* **choice**) between the ego and the Holy Spirit. Not the **ego**, for the ego is only an idea in your mind, a self-concept you have mistaken for yourself. It is not real and cannot be redeemed. Not the **Christ**, strictly speaking, for the Christ cannot fall asleep. However, since in Heaven part and whole are one, the part of you that is asleep and dreaming is one with your entire Self, the Christ. It is already perfect and redeemed. *See* T-6.IV.6.

About the Author

Robert Perry has been a student of *A Course in Miracles* (ACIM) since 1981. He taught at Miracle Distribution Center in California from 1986 to 1989, and in 1993 founded the Circle of Atonement in Sedona, Arizona. The Circle is an organization composed of several teachers dedicated to helping establish the Course as an authentic spiritual tradition.

One of the most respected voices on ACIM, Robert has traveled extensively, speaking throughout the U.S. and internationally. In addition to contributing scores of articles to various Course publications, he is the author or co-author of twenty books and booklets, including *Path of Light: Stepping into Peace with* A Course in Miracles. Robert's goal has always been to provide a complete picture of what the Course is—as a thought system and as a path meant to be lived in the world on a daily basis—and to support students in walking along that path.

www.circlepublishing.org

Circle Publishing is a division of the
Circle of Atonement Teaching and Healing Center.

The Circle of Atonement offers a wide range of teaching materials
designed to help the student walk the transformative path of
A Course in Miracles. It offers a vision of the Course that is both
faithful to it and practical for the student. Visit the Circle's website
at www.circleofa.org for a wealth of free materials, including
articles by Robert Perry, Daily Lesson Commentaries by Allen
Watson, and Course Q&A's by Greg Mackie. You may also sign
up to receive the Circle's free e-newsletter, *A Better Way*, or to
receive Allen's Lesson Commentaries or Robert's weekly class
notes by e-mail.

Contact:
The Circle of Atonement
P.O. Box 4238
West Sedona, AZ 86340
Phone: (928) 282 0790
E-mail: info@circleofa.org
www.circleofa.org